In eight years of Sparkman's proposal is t] judicial problems I have heard.
Tom Valentine
Radio Free America

As a long time lay volunteer and oberver of our U.S. criminal justice system, I feel that Richard Sparkman's book, through his experience, vision, creative thinking and selfless approach, makes a major contribution to potential correction of major faults which harm society and individuals.
Robert Stuart
Past President Chicago Crime Commission
Past Chairman National Association of Citizen Crime Commissions
Past Vice Chairman National Council on Crime and Delinquency
Founding Director National Crime Prevention Council
Chairman Emeritus National Can Corporation

Congratulations on an excellent piece of work.
Rep. Jerry Melvin
Florida House of Representatives

Of the books I have reviewed, <u>Failed Justice</u> holds the most promising solution for America's faltering legal system.
Gary Roen
Book Editor
Halifax Magazine

<u>Failed Justice</u> doesn't suggest we reform the legal system, it suggests we replace it.
The Lake Worth Herald

I am proud of your accomplishment and I am MOST IMPRESSED.
The Honorable Doctor Richard Bivins Lansdale
Naples, Florida

I am glad to finally see an attorney who told the truth.
Edmund D. Mann
Professor of Paralegal Studies
Centereach, NY

The Edison Society is pleased to inform you that you have been selected to receive the Edison Society "Excellence in Innovation" award.
Thomas E. Hughs
Founder and President

Sparkman is a man with a message.
News Press
Ft. Myers, Florida

Failed Justice is a remarkable piece of work.
Marcus A. Brown
St. Louis, Mo.

The ideas expressed in Failed Justice have merit.
Hon. Paul E. Rink
Chief Judge, Retired
Rock Island, ILL

As director of Public Affairs for a top FM Adult Contemporary Radio station in a major market I garner a lot of information and understanding by conversing with a very wide range of people . . . enough to fill 5 programs per week. One of the things I've come to learn is that understanding our system of justice is something of a challenge for most of us. Nevertheless it is something most, if not all, of us believe needs some modification. "Failed Justice . . . America's Faltering Legal System" addresses both these. Before identifying and/or addressing what's wrong with "the system" we must first have a pretty good understanding of it that goes beyond the surface. What Richard Sparkman's "Failed Justice . . . " has managed to do is provide insight/education regarding our trial system so that we as a society can recognize and address its ills.

Naomi Wright-Warren
Director, Public Affairs
Jefferson Pilot Communications
WLYF/WMXJ/WAXY
Miami, Florida

Most interesting reading and a true insight into our Justice System.

Henry Harms
Rupert, Idaho

Failed Justice is interesting, thought provoking, and well written.

Mrs. Herbert J. Motley
North Haven, Maine

Failed Justice tells my story of a middle-income citizen caught in the financial meat grinder of the American legal system. Sparkman tells us how we can change the system, and we should listen.

Diane,
A victim of failed justice.

Calling it as he sees it, Sparkman states, "... It is a pity that we have a legal system in which creating an illusion or falsehood for a jury is venerated." Sparkman doesn't mince words: "Any system based on the art of deceiving the trier of fact, the judge or the jury, and giving the advantage to an unscrupulous lawyer and his lying client is fatally flawed." His book is an excellent layman's look at today's justice.

Marti Martindale,
Freelance writer

Having been taught that the legal system is fair and the recourse of choice in times of dispute, I have become disillusioned after experiences which have shown the exact opposite. As Mr. Sparkman so ably points out, the system not only favors but rewards those who operate without conscience. This book should be required reading in every high school government or civics class in the country.

Paul A. Long, MS
Family Therapis

Our courts cannot control our ciminals and our civil dockets are out of control. Sooner or later we are going to have to change our trial system. When we do, the changes will have to be similar to what Sparkman proposes in **Failed Justice.**

In *Failed Justice*, Sparkman takes a hard look at our faltering legal system. After working inside the legal system for over twenty years, he has a profound knowledge of how the system works (or doesn't work), and powerful insight as to how it might be fixed. Sparkman asserts it is time for Americans to look the cannon in the mouth and understand that we need to abandon an antiquated and cumbrson adversarial jury trial system. A shocking and riveting critique of one of our most important institutions.

© Copyright 1997

All rights reserved. No part of this book may be reproduced without permission from the publisher, except by a reviewer who may quote brief passages in a review; nor may any part of this book be reproduced, stored in a retrieval system, or copied by mechanical, photocopying, recording or other means, without permission from the publisher.

First edition 1996

Library of Congress Card Catalogue Number:
96-90719
ISBN - 0-9653780-0-4
Precision Prep & Press, Inc. & Image Marketing

Easterly Publishing, Inc.
307 Airport Road N.
Naples, Florida 34104

FAILED JUSTICE

A SOLUTION FOR AMERICA'S FALTERING LEGAL SYSTEM

Second Edition

Richard D. Sparkman
ATTORNEY AT LAW

EASTERLY PUBLISHING, INC.
NAPLES, FLORIDA

DEDICATION

In loving memory of my father, Guy Raymond Sparkman; and for my mother, Helen Erline Sparkman; and my brother, Robert Scott Sparkman.

ACKNOWLEDGMENTS

My first debt is to my long-time friend Edna McAlexander, advisor and editor. I express my appreciation to my friend and legal associate, counselor-at-law Karen Beavin, who helped me to clarify concepts, corrected the early drafts, and subdued my immoderation. My friend David Millich, advised, encouraged, and provided computer assistance.

My son, Eric Sparkman, assisted with his computer skills; and my daughter, Cassandra Sparkman, helped with the word processor.

My secretary, Teena J. Ley, managed the totality of my affairs as she has so capably for many years. My secretaries, Clara Parr, Lynn Johnson, and Mary Wingrove, assisted in logistics.

I am deeply indebted to my friend and law partner of many years, Jeffrey C. Quinn, who acted as my chief discourager. He constantly admonishes me to quit wasting time writing books and to practice law.

"Trial by jury, instead of being a security to persons who are accused, will be a delusion, a mockery, and a snare."

> Lord Denman Thomas
> *O'Connell v. The Queen*
> September 4, 1844[1]

CONTENTS

PREFACE	XIII
FOREWORD	XV
INTRODUCTION	XIX
PART I: WHAT'S WRONG	1
CHAPTER 1: The Adversarial Trial System	3
Show Business	7
CHAPTER II: Trial by Jury	17
A Miscarriage of Justice	23
Phil	30
CHAPTER III: The Unaffordable System	41
Diane	44
CHAPTER IV: Business	55
Contractor	60
CHAPTER V: Personal Injury	67
Wendy	72
CHAPTER VI: Family Law	81
Fred and Arlene	84
CHAPTER VII: The Criminal Justice System	89
Charley	96
PART II: THE PLAYERS	105
CHAPTER VIII: Lawyers	107
CHAPTER IX: Judges	115
Jack's House	117
Personality Disorder	124

CHAPTER X: Bar Associations	133
PART III: STRUCTURE AND PROCEDURE	137
CHAPTER XI: Court Structure	139
CHAPTER XII: Law and Procedure	143
CHAPTER XIII: Questions of Evidence	147
PART IV: HOW TO FIX IT	155
CHAPTER XIV: Civil Non-Adversarial Proceedings	157
CHAPTER XV: Criminal Non-Adversarial Proceedings and the Constitutional Problem	163
CHAPTER XVI: The Consequences of Change	169
Judges	170
Personal Injury	171
Business	173
Citizens	174
CHAPTER XVII: Privatization	175
CHAPTER XVIII: Caveat	179
EPILOGUE	183
APPENDIX I	187
APPENDIX II	189
APPENDIX III	193
APPENDIX IV	197
AFTERWORD	199

PREFACE

The examples used within are from the laws and courts of Florida. This is where the author practices, and it is the law with which he is most familiar. For the purposes of this book, the name of any state can be substituted, as the laws of the several states are almost identical.

This book is not gender specific except for actual examples. Gender choices throughout the book are for the convenience of the reader only. The illustrative stories in this book are true. Some situations have been combined or names and scenery changed to disguise the identities.

FOREWORD

"One word often overlooked in discussing the civil justice system is the word *civil*," Supreme Court Justice Sandra Day O'Connor told an American Bar Association conference in December of 1993.[2] She went on to tell the conference that lawyers would better serve their clients by being more civil and less combative. She cited others who predicted that the practice of law in the 1990s would be nasty and brutish and that technology would be no panacea.

Supreme Court Justice Harry Blackmun, articulating his opposition to the death penalty in February 1994, stated:

> From this day forward, I no longer shall tinker with the machinery of death. For more than twenty years I have endeavored—indeed, I have struggled—along with the majority of this Court, to develop procedural and substantive rules that would lend more than the mere appearance of fairness to the death penalty endeavor. Rather than continue to coddle the Court's delusion that the desired level of fairness has been achieved and the need for regulation eviscerated, I feel morally and intellectually obligated simply

to concede that the death penalty experiment has failed. It is virtually self-evident to me now that no combination of procedural rules or substantive regulations ever can save the death penalty from its inherent Constitutional deficiencies. The basic question—does the system accurately and consistently determine which defendants "deserve" to die?—cannot be answered in the affirmative. It is not simply that this Court has allowed vague aggravating circumstances to be employed, relevant mitigating evidence to be disregarded, and vital judicial review to be blocked. The problem is that the inevitability of factual, legal, and moral error gives us a system that we know must wrongly kill some defendants, a system that fails to deliver the fair, consistent, and reliable sentences of death required by the Constitution.[3]

While I do not contend that either Justice Blackmun or Justice O'Connor is saying that something is fundamentally wrong with the American legal system, I detect a hint of uneasiness.

This hint of a fundamental problem in our legal system is not new. The laws of the United States of America Title 28, United States Code Annotated, Federal Rules of Civil Procedure, dated 10 December 1991, start with an "Explanation." The "Explanation" discusses the rules that were promulgated over fifty years ago for the United States district courts, and it says in part:

> Their durability and wide acceptance are a tribute to the framers whose primary objectives were to ensure access to justice and provide for the just and speedy determination of claims. Remaining substantially intact over the years, recent developments have called into question the continued effectiveness of the Rules. The proliferation of attorneys, the interstate and international nature of American business and culture, and social philosophy that encourages litigation have led to an overwhelming number of civil cases instituted in the Federal district courts. The congested court dockets, extensive delays, large awards and settlements, and soaring expenses that have resulted threaten the viability of the

Federal civil justice system. Today, many litigants and lawyers turn to alternative methods of conflict resolution while the Federal judiciary and Congress deal with the realities of practices and procedures under the Rules through ongoing oversight and revision.[4]

My interpretation of this statement is that the Rules were written over fifty years ago to make a faltering American federal civil-justice system work. They succeeded for fifty years, but the federal legal system is again under stress because of the many changes in American society. This incipient failure is recognized by the legal profession and the many litigants who are turning to alternate conflict-resolution methods such as mediation and dispute-resolution centers. Congress and the federal judiciary keep reshuffling and "band-aiding," or repairing, the American judicial system in an effort to make it work.

I contend they have failed and will continue to fail. The state courts are in even worse shape. I further contend that the trial courts, at both state and federal levels, are failing in their assigned functions of providing our citizens with equal protection of the laws. The explanation of why the American legal systems are failing and what can be done about them will be revealed in this book.

INTRODUCTION

The United States of America has impressive legal facilities. We have a large body of law with well-reasoned decisions covering a multitude of subjects. Our legal fundamentals are solid and based on noble legal principles. The system is dynamic with legislative and judicial capabilities to adjust, amend, and refine the laws as circumstances require. Our administrative wherewithal is vast, attended by an army of skilled workers in ample facilities. We have thousands of educated, well-intentioned judges and millions of similarly disposed lawyers. Existent are all the ingredients to brew a great legal system—most of it is pretty good. The problem is, there is something fundamentally wrong with the American legal system.

Witness: Crime plagues America, and we do not know what to do about it. Our citizens grit their teeth in despair at silly verdicts in showcase trials. Many businesses are stifled because of exorbitant product-liability awards while others have been destroyed. Personal-injury awards, viewed nationwide, are grossly unfair. Trials are frequently little better than lying contests won by technicalities or a lawyer's show-business skills. The system is too complex for citizens to use without the help of expensive legal representation. Clients pay too much for these legal services, and the product is often of poor quality, even with the best representation. Lawyers are losing the confidence and respect of the public. The lawyers are as disgusted as the public, and many would quit, given a reasonable alternative.

The public has but a theatrical understanding of the legal system and is rightfully afraid of it. The American legal system is a horse-and-buggy system born and nurtured in a rural eighteenth-century society. It is not performing in our urban-communication civilization. The legal system of America, euphemistically referred to as a justice system, does not work very well.

The inadequacy of our legal system has not gone unrecognized. The reform of the Federal Rules of Civil Procedure, now fifty years past, was an implicit acknowledgment of its initial failures. The "Explanation" at the beginning of Title 28, United States Code Annotated, is a renewed acknowledgment that something is wrong.

Justice Blackmun's unsuccessful twenty-year struggle to develop procedures to lend fairness to only one area of the law warns us that other areas may be equally unfair.[5]

Annually, modifications and reforms pour forth from legislative assemblies and supreme courts. These changes do not work very well, either. They act as band-aids on a failing system.

Introduction

We have not seen the weaknesses in the system because we have not looked. Our preeminent success as a nation has lulled us into complacency about this fundamental institution. We do not doubt the rightness of our legal system; therefore, we do not question it.

Crime in the streets, high legal costs, and bloated court dockets are the price we pay for our reluctance to look at the guts of the legal system. It is time to look the cannon in the mouth and examine the very fundamentals. Upon doing so, we will see an adversarial jury system, garnished by a single omnipotent judge, that has outlived its best days, requiring modernization and change. This book will first define the problem, then discuss how the American legal system affects various populations, business people, accident victims, criminals, and people who work in and for the system. Next, we will outline the structure of the system. Finally, we will talk about what needs to be done to give America a legal system that better serves our citizens and more closely meets the promise of the Constitution—the equal protection of the laws.

I am advocating four significant changes that are necessarily interrelated. The most important change will be to abolish the adversarial approach to trials and replace it with a problem-solving approach. Next, I suggest that we abandon the system of trial by jury and the single-judge system, replacing them with bifurcated trials presided over by three judges. Finally, I suggest we abandon the exclusionary rule.

Reforming the American legal system will not be easy, nor will change find ready acceptance. Our system has deep historical roots in English common law, and it is welded into our civilization by the Bill of Rights in our Constitution and the constitutions of the several states.

The changes I am advocating will be among the most fundamental changes in this government since the Constitution of the United States became effective on the first Wednesday in March 1789.

1. John Bartlett, *Familiar Quotations*. Ed. Emily Morison Beck. 15th ed. Boston: Little, Brown and Company. 1980: 445.
2. Sandra Day O'Connor. Associate Justice Supreme Court of the United States. "Civil Justice System Improvements." American Bar Association. Washington, D. C. 15 Dec. 1993.
3. *Callins v. Collins*. 93-7054. Supreme Court. 1994.
4. US Code. Title 28. 1991.
5. *Callins v. Collins*.

PART I

WHAT'S WRONG

CHAPTER I

THE ADVERSARIAL TRIAL SYSTEM

The main problem with the American legal system, the primary reason it is not working very well, is the nature of the trial system itself. It is an adversarial trial system. Adversarial in the context of hostility, antipathy, contrariness, and even repugnance; adversarial with a capital "A." The purpose of a trial court is to peacefully resolve disputes and problems. To best accomplish this objective, the primary focus of the court system must be on solving problems and disputes. The primary focus of our adversarial trial system, however, is on winning cases, not on solving problems. The very word "adversarial" establishes a tone and vocabulary that render the legal system into an environment of verbal conflict and hostility, the antithesis of efficient dispute resolution. Historically, disputes and problems are more efficiently resolved through a process that encourages or requires cooperation and a search for common ground rather than through conflict. Even the international community understands that conflict and war are economically inefficient problem-solving methods.

We Americans, in spite of historical lessons and psychological studies, maintain a conflict system to solve our criminal and civil trial-court problems. The violence in our society suggests a regression to an ancient dispute-resolution method: war. Our legal system is a modified system of combat called a trial.

Let me illustrate how the system works: Lawyer A takes a position, and lawyer B takes an opposite or different position. The lawyers duel with words rather than swords or pistols. The field of honor is the courtroom with the rules of court and the rules of evidence to limit the maneuvers. The judge acts as a referee while the court clerks, bailiffs, and others act as seconds to the participants. The clients hold the honorable position of victim.

The theory is that from this cauldron of conflict and fiery words the truth will emerge, just like on *Perry Mason*. If lawyer A presents all of his evidence, based on the rules, and lawyer B presents all of his evidence, the judge or the jury will be able to discern who is telling the truth and who is lying; or, if both sides are equal, who is more equal.

Once in a while this system actually works. The theory sounds great and looks good on paper; mathematically, it should work. Thus, the equation: when A clashes with B, T (truth) emerges.

The reality is generally quite different. In an adversarial trial system the focus is skewed from the problem or the client to the actual combatants—the lawyers. They become the primary participants; and their skills, training, and character become paramount. The trial becomes a contest between lawyers, frequently a bitter contest, sometimes an acting contest; it is only incidentally a dispute-resolution forum and often creates more problems than it solves.

A citizen with a problem or dispute enters a law office and relates the situation to the lawyer. At that point, the primary participant is the citizen, who must communicate with the lawyer to initiate the process. Once the citizen retains the lawyer, the citizen then becomes a client. Now a "client," the citizen is almost incidental as the lawyer takes over virtually exclusive management of the problem.

The lawyer becomes the primary participant in the legal process when he or she drafts the first documents or pleadings and commences the lawsuit by having the opponent served with process. To address, modify, amend, or challenge these initial pleadings, the lawyers engage in what is referred to as "motion practice." The lawyers make motions asking the court for rulings and orders, which direct the progress of the lawsuit. The lawyers are still the primary participants as the clients generally do not participate at this stage.

Discovery, the next stage in a lawsuit, is the process by which the attorneys obtain information about the opponent's case. They may use interrogatories, written questions, depositions, or several other methods authorized by the rules. The clients are involved in this process only as information sources, and the lawyers may even attempt to limit client participation. In some cases client participation is limited by court rules.[1] As in the other stages, the attorney is the primary participant.

As the case progresses, the parties' positions have a tendency to polarize and harden. Lawyers become more partisan and may begin to tear at each other until the client's interest is lost in conflict. Few clients understand what is taking place, and therefore they are unable to stop the escalation of the conflict until all hope of resolution or reconciliation is lost. The whole process is the very antithesis of rational problem solving.

The trial is almost exclusively a lawyer's show. At trial, the client's participation may increase, depending on his attorney's desire for increased participation. In state court trials the lawyer's function begins with jury selection. This selection is almost totally the lawyer's responsibility, the client being limited to a word here and there with his attorney.

Once testimony starts, the client is a witness only if need be. The client, whose money or freedom is on the line, is along for the ride, or else taken for a ride, depending on the situation. The important point is that the clients are ancillary participants, not the main show, even though it is their posteriors on the line. Summation, or closing argument, to the jury is exclusively a lawyer's duty, and again it can be all show business. Instruction to the jury is the judge's show; and, of course, deliberation and decision belong to the jury.

Throughout the legal process the primary participant is the lawyer. "So what?" asks the sophisticated reader. "Isn't that the lawyer's job? Is not the skill or knowledge of a person what defines a professional?" The answer is "Yes." A patient must certainly rely on the skill of his surgeon. Comparably, the courtroom is an operating room with two surgeons; however, while one is trying to save the patient, the other is using his skills to kill him.

Continuing the medical analogy, it is fair to observe that like the client in the courtroom, the patient is not an active participant in the operating room. The courtroom, however, is very different. It is primarily a communication forum whereas the operating room is not.

Thirty years ago a Canadian professor, Marshall McLuhan, in his book *Understanding Media*, taught us that the "Medium is the Message," the title of his first chapter.[2] The "medium" in the courtroom is the lawyer. Even lawyer movies and television sitcoms focus on the lawyer to the exclusion of the client. Clients are little more than props in the entertainment industry. Unfortunately the adversary system makes clients little more than props in the real courtrooms of our country.

The "message" in American courtrooms is the adversarial legal process. This adversarial process sets the tone and the environment of the American trial system. In this system the fundamental process is conflict, combat, and disagreement rather than compromise, reconciliation, and problem solving. This combative concept renders the whole American trial system expensive and inefficient. It hampers every level and division of the trial courts of our country. Because of this adversarial process, the criminal-justice system is failing, and the "little people" cannot afford to utilize the system for protection from the big people.

As Justice Sandra Day O'Connor observed, there is an increasing brutishness and nastiness in the practice of law in America.[3] Adversarial problem solving in a fast-paced communication society is going to become nastier, more brutish, more inefficient, and inevitably prohibitively expensive.

If we do not change from a combative-adversarial system of law to a non-adversarial system, our courtrooms will become obsolete battlegrounds, serious problem solving will be usurped by private enterprise, and our alienated citizens will solve their problems with violence. The proper attire for a mid-twenty-first-century judge may be a bomb suit.

Show Business

Timothy's case is representative of the concept that the American trial court is occasionally little more than a lawyer's stage for show business, and we all know there is "no business like show business." The client is only along for an expensive ride. I met Tim after I had been practicing criminal trial law five years, give or take. I was good at it—young, enthusiastic, and smart. I had the natural instincts of a good cross-examiner and ambusher. My brain, now slowing with the caution age teaches, processed information with lightning speed; it did this while its owner was on his feet, and it was not afraid to gamble. Not many gambles were lost. In addition to tactics, I had begun to formulate concepts about the criminal-trial courtroom that would be universal truths and always give me the advantage.

Benjamin—we were to call him Ben—filled in my perception of what the American courtroom, too frequently, is all about. He was one of America's premier criminal-trial lawyers. Several books to his credit, he was considered an authority on the entire envelope of criminal law. It is the only time in my career I have had the opportunity to work in conjunction with one of America's super lawyers.

Early one Monday evening I received a telephone call from a colleague, a civil lawyer, who had a business client charged with a crime. Would I like to discuss the case with them on the morrow and lead the defense, there being adequate funds available? Of course I would.

At the appointed time, I was ushered into my friend's office to meet the pleasant, well-dressed businessman I will call Timothy. Tim had expanded his business enterprises to include pornography. He was retailing Swedish erotic films (no video tapes at that time) and triple-X magazines. The laws of the state were less tolerant a few years ago, and the local community was completely intolerant. Tim was facing some significant prison time, and he was, understandably, concerned.

My colleague and I filed the appropriate pleadings and dove into the law books to understand the state laws and the United States Supreme Court decisions on obscenity. After considerable struggle we recognized that the laws were vague and that we knew little more than when we had started. Our inability to provide Timothy with definitive answers to his questions frightened him. He began to cast around for someone who seemed to know what he was doing.

Benjamin came winging into our community to meet Tim and his defense team. He was not replacing my colleague and me. "No, no, absolutely not." He would need local counsel to do the spadework while he directed the case, from afar, to appear only for the significant battles and subsequently, Armageddon.

This pleasant, patrician gentlemen assured us he had checked up on us and we were highly respected trial lawyers. We accepted the accolades and were eager to be retained on the case, promising to work closely with Ben and under his direction. On later reflection, we realized he had done no such thing; he had not investigated us with anybody. After the evening dinner and drinks, having urged us to stay on, he had acquired sufficient information to determine that Tim had not hired a couple of idiots and that we would suffice for his understudies and vassals.

A more pleasant, soft-spoken, or hospitable man would be hard to find. We discussed the case in general and planned for a technical hearing scheduled a month hence. We were to research the law and prepare a brief for Ben; he would fly in and make the argument. Our searching, substantive questions were deflected: he would be in touch, and all would be answered in due time.

When Ben boarded the plane to leave, my friend and I had no more information about the law of the case or where we were going with it than the moment Ben had deplaned. Oh, well, Ben was such a pleasant man, and we were sure the maestro would reveal his strategy at the proper moment.

My friend and I went back to the books and came up with the same confusing results. We telephoned and corresponded with Ben, followed his guidance, and tried to answer his inquires. By the time we wrote Ben's courtroom brief, on a very narrow technical legal question, we knew no more than we did before Ben was retained. We realized the material in the brief was bad at best and nonsense at worst. We were concerned that

Ben would be disappointed in our efforts and maybe even critical.

Quite the contrary. Ben returned for the hearing with the same stately demeanor that had already charmed the savage in our souls, and he generously praised our efforts. He granted absolution for our failure to find satisfactory answers to all the legal questions we had been commissioned to find. That no answers existed anywhere in the law to some of the questions was unknown to us. Ben already knew. He had done this drill before.

That hearing was my first introduction to big-time show-business criminal-trial law. Benjamin advanced across the courtroom and regally presented the arguments from our brief, almost verbatim. He did not deviate, he did not innovate, he did not supplement. He dramatically presented the thin logic my friend and I had come up with to address this legal issue.

During Ben's theatrical display, the prosecutor could hardly contain himself. A bright, no-nonsense guy, he could not believe this apex of American trial law was pouring such verbal nonsense all over the bench. The judge understood what was going on and was more amused than incensed. An intelligent man, he was enjoying this show-business diversion from his normal fare. He quickly waved off the prosecutor's objections and allowed Ben to roll unhampered into a booming conclusion.

My friend and I looked at each other and secretly rolled our eyes. The press—someone had surreptitiously notified them—ate it up. We came to find out Ben had a public relations manager. The prosecutor's response was so shrill we thought he had been emasculated. Needless to say, the judge denied our motion.

My friend and I were ready to slink away and hide under our desks. Not so with Ben: he was just getting started. He effusively praised the Court's wisdom to the point that the judge actually began to show embarrassment. I thought the prosecutor was going to throw up.

When he finished fawning all over the judge, Ben turned his charm on the prosecutor. He firmly grasped the prosecutor's hand. The prosecutor, who apparently did not want Ben to touch him, flinched and tried to get away. Ben would not let him go. In soft but sincere terms he apologized to the prosecutor and asked for his understanding. It was necessary for the mental health of his client that he make argument on each issue. Ben knew his argument was spurious and hoped the prosecutor would understand. Ben did not let go until the prosecutor assured him he understood.

Ben then turned to the press. They wanted a picture. Sure. Ben draped his arm around Tim and whispered in his ear to smile and pose for the reporters. Ben then granted individual interviews to each of the reporters after giving a dramatic statement to the television press. He pontificated on guilt or innocence and the American way of justice; Ben carried the flag.

My friend and I were dismayed. We had been taught in ethics that a lawyer did not try a case in the press nor comment on substantive matters while the case was in progress. In fact, there were disciplinary rules specifically forbidding such conduct. Ben was not dismayed. That was all nonsense, a rule all big leaguers ignored, and had we ever heard of anyone disciplined for commenting to the press? Ben liked us: time for our first lesson.

Trial law? (smile) This is show business. Always give the press a statement; potential jurors may be listening and may be subliminally influenced. Make sure you give the photographers the shot they want. Never let your client look like a criminal or look guilty. Never, never, never let your client be caught hiding his face. Control the pose and the picture. Hide the handcuffs, make sure the shot is of your best side, and have your client smiling innocently and handsomely for the photographers.

"Look what happened here. We lost in the courtroom, but we will win in the press. We had nothing in the courtroom, but the press will write favorable copy. The electronic media will edit all but the dramatic remarks and give us an upbeat review," Ben lectured. Sure enough, by the time the media finished with their articles, Ben looked as though he was marching toward a glorious victory for law and justice.

Ben never ceased to amaze us. We lost every hearing, and our position was hopeless as we moved ever closer to trial. All legal avenues were closed, but we were winning big in the press. Eventually there came a day of reckoning. It was either settle the case or go to trial. All thoughts of trial were terrifying.

We had had a field day seeking community standards. We had set up a small movie studio in our office and were inviting one and all to view the Swedish erotica and give us their opinion as to community standards and acceptability. Our cheerful judge had also retained a copy of the entire collection for judicial review. (Nobody ever managed to retrieve those copies, and it was not brought up to the judge. Years later, when I asked him what happened to them, he clapped me on the back, telling me they were still under judicial review.)

Of course, we knew the elderly retirees in our community were not likely to acquit Tim after viewing heterosexual, homosexual, group, and interracial sex in the Swedish erotica. It was the new culture, alien and repugnant to them.

Ben did not appear concerned as we walked into the courtroom for trial. My friend did not expect to play any role in the trial, but I was apprehensive. Ben had played his cards closely and evaded all inquires about a division of labor in the courtroom. I tried to prepare for the worst, thinking Mr. Show Business might well throw his vassals to the wolves when the going got tough.

I began studying the jury list and setting up shop. Ben caught my eye, smiled, and distinctly said, "Showtime." He then cloistered himself with the prosecutor. I knew he was trying to cut a deal, but I did not know how far he would go. I had little hope for success; I knew how far the prosecutor would go, and that was not very far. I could see Ben doing most of the talking and the prosecutor shaking his head "no."

Ben had made no progress with the prosecution by the time the judge arrived in the courtroom to begin the trial. Ben was on his feet immediately, asking the judge to convene a conference between the attorneys before beginning the trial. The prosecutor objected, but the judge, almost always amenable to avoiding a time-consuming trial, agreed.

Once in chambers, Ben grabbed center stage by diverting the conversation from the subject at hand to a general discussion of law and the notorious cases in which he had been involved. The prosecutor sat through this show patiently. Ben eventually guided the conversation to the desirability of always settling cases versus trying them. The judge launched into his own dissertation on the desirability of settling while the minutes and the morning trial time wasted away. I was almost snoozing when Ben told the judge we would like to explain our position, and Mr. Sparkman would handle that chore.

I was shocked into consciousness but managed to pick up the ball and present a reasonable proposition to the judge. The judge liked what he was hearing, but the prosecution wanted no part of it. Ben grabbed the ball again and went into another dissertation about how good judges controlled events and encouraged him to lean on the prosecution. He did. The prosecution was not moving very much, so the judge suggested we troop over to the chief prosecutor's office and ask him to lean on his subordinate.

The chief prosecutor was reluctant to push his subordinate around, but we managed to come up with a deal a little short of prison. The judge was delighted, so we entered a plea that was less than what a jury guilty verdict would bring but far too much for the offense had we not escalated this case to a *cause celebre* in the press. Since this was a pornography case, everybody involved realized it was a political case from the beginning. In any case, Tim was willing to accept the deal.

We had expected a three-to-five-day trial, but not Ben. His return tickets were for late the first day of trial, and he had always known he would make the plane. Ben knew he was going to take the state's best offer. He already had his fee. Tim, exhausted, gathered up his family and went home. My friend and I drove Ben to the airport after an enlightening lunch. He did not expect to be in this area again, nor was it likely we would ever have the opportunity to work with him again. He was more than willing to do a postmortem and tell us how he functioned.

He laughed when we mentioned his books. "Write them?" He had not even read them. Students had written them, and knowledgeable associates had proofread them. He put his name on the books for the royalties. Try a case? That was even funnier. Ben was not in the criminal trial business: he was in show business. He never tried cases. He did not even know how to try a case. Heaven forbid he should ever get stuck in a situation like that.

He was greatly amused with himself. He was one of America's premier criminal-trial lawyers, celebrated in print and the electronic media, and did not even know how to actually try an entire case. He thought the whole idea was great fun. His technique was to scope the local bar association and select, if not the best defense lawyer available, at least a good one. If worse came to worst, that lawyer would try the case with Ben giving the opening and closing arguments. In Ben's case

Failed Justice

the arguments were more theatrical than judicial, and he cheerfully acknowledged the fact, in private.

Ben's forte was being a celebrity. He did the talk-show circuit, put his name on books and articles written by others, and collected tremendous fees because of his celebrity status. His primary goal in the defense of criminals was to make money. If he occasionally won a case, that was okay too. If he lost, by the time it was retried in the press, it looked as if Ben had won after all. In any case, he rarely worked the same area twice. He was a delightful phony who took his client's money and provided little more than a legal opera for his fee. If the court did not punish the criminals, he did, and justice prevailed.

I have not been involved in a legal circus of this sort since I worked with Ben, but I see a world of it going on in American courts. We Americans should be ashamed that our halls of justice are arenas for these circuses. We need a better system.

My evaluation on Tim's case is that the courtroom is a lawyer's show; it has little to do with the client-victims, and many citizens are flim-flammed. Once Ben started the show-business stuff, the prosecution hardened its position and became more adversarial and virtually intractable. Everybody made out like a bandit except Tim. Tim paid a fortune for his legal opera and probably received a heavier sentence than we could have quietly negotiated without Ben. At least I have always believed that and have maintained my eternal skepticism toward super-show-business lawyers and the circuses they conduct.

Tim's case and the other cases in this book are for entertainment as well as illustrative pruposes. These cases aside, I wish to emphasize that the primary objective of this book is to impress upon the reader that it is the adversary process in our courtrooms that has resulted in our failing trial system. It is for the reader to understand that ours is a four-hundred-year experiment in the use of a trial concept, the adversarial system, that has proven itself unable to control our criminals and unable to provide our citizens with the Constitutional promise of equal protection of the laws. It is not a question of the abolishment or retention of the jury system, the merits of election versus the appointment of judges, the number of judges, or any of a host of proffered solutions. It is more fundamental; our experiment with the adversarial system has failed. Let us recognize this unfortunate circumstance, scrap the adversarial concept, and build a new trial system. Any other reform is a waste of time and a squandering of our national energy.

I invite the legislatures of America to test this argument by immediately passing every bar association-sponsored reform intended to make the adversarial system work. I prophesy that all of the reforms will fail absolutely, that America's trial systems will not work one whit better and will be ever more dysfunctional.

Notes:

1. *Florida Rules of Criminal Procedure. Rule 3.220(h)(6).*
2. *Marshall McLuhan. "Medium Is the Message."* Understanding Media. *McGraw-Hill. New York. 1964.*
3. *Jonathan L. Kirsch, "Times Will Get Tougher for Litigators," California Lawyer, Date, 40-42. Quoted by Sandra Day O'Connor.*

CHAPTER II

TRIAL BY JURY

One of the most sacred of our fundamental institutions is trial by jury. As Americans we are proud of this institution and believe it is the cornerstone of the best and fairest legal system in the world. Unfortunately most Americans are wrong. The jury-trial system of dispute resolution is one of the primary reasons Justice Blackmun and his colleagues have been unable to find substantive or procedural rules that will make death cases fair.[1] The jury-trial system is second only to the adversarial process in responsibility for the incipient failure of American court systems. Having represented clients from other countries, I have found that many of these clients look at our jury-trial system far more critically than we do. Some see it as simply inefficient; others view it as antiquated and unfair.

Trial by jury is guaranteed to our citizens by the United States Constitution.

The jury system of trial served colonial America and the young republic adequately. America was a rural, agricultural society. Most of the people were farmers or served those who worked the land. These farmers, the free men, were literate and racially and culturally similar. For the most part, early America was a homogeneous population. The founding fathers lived in this environment when they were framing the Constitution.

To place our thinking in perspective, it helps if we recognize that early American technology was more like the classical civilizations of Greece and Rome than like contemporary American technology. The classical civilizations had only human and animal power. America had little more when our founding fathers wrote the Constitution. The spoken word and the written word were the communication technology, and most people used oil or candles for illumination.

The population of early America was small compared to today's population, and most people in any given community knew each other. The lawyers and professionals generally knew each other, knew the good people, and knew the criminals.

The subject matter of civil lawsuits in early America was either a minor contract dispute or a disgreement concerning the ownership and use of land. Most of our basic legal precedents were brought from England. The rest were established during the colonial and early national periods based mainly on land disputes.

To contrast America of the 1990s with classical Greece is to note the staggering difference between present-day America and the America that developed our jury system.

We are the great melting pot; however, we no longer know each other, or our professionals, or our good people, or our criminals, or even our next-door neighbor. We are strangers in a strange land becoming further estranged. Our technology, communications, transportation, medicine, and just about everything else, except our legal system, bear little resemblance to early America. In spite of this we do not question this early American institution. It is time for us to look closely at how it is functioning today.

Jury trials in early America were community events compared to today's trial; they were relatively rare, and the subject matter was not complex. Judges rode a circuit, hence the title *circuit judge*. The jurors often knew the participants from litigants to lawyers to judges and probably had some community knowledge of the issues before them.

Today's juror arrives for jury duty among strangers. The juror can expect to be taken to a courtroom where he or she will be addressed by lawyers he does not know, in front of a judge he does not know, for litigants he does not know, about a subject that may be completely baffling.

The educational and cultural differences of people sitting on juries today are enormous. At first glance, this would appear to be an advantage in a world where the subject matter before juries is as diverse and complex as the society itself. This diversity on the jury is not necessarily good. If one person on the jury has some expertise in the subject matter presented, that person becomes the jury's expert, and his or her arguments tend to dominate the jury deliberations. If we accept that each juror brings to the courthouse his or her prejudices and maybe an agenda, then that juror's agenda will be served even if it is unfair or wrong. This is, in fact, what happens in a large number of cases. These prejudices and agendas are the concerns of jury-selection experts. These experts study the potential jurors, their backgrounds, education, and other cultural factors to predict how they will view the case and the litigants who will appear before them. Lawyers attempt to use this information to an advantage by playing to juror prejudices or picking jurors who will be favorably disposed toward their client's cause or situation. These people have worked to reduce jury selection to a science. For the most part, they have failed and will continue to fail. Juries are too diverse and fickle to be understood scientifically. Verdicts are occasionally controlled by the juror who is the most opinionated or, heaven forbid, even the dumbest.

In most cases, a jury trial is mandatory if one party's attorney demands it. Lawyers know the advantages and disadvantages of the jury trial over a trial before a single judge. If the judge's prejudices or working philosophies are not favorable to the attorney's case, he or she is prudent to opt for a jury trial. More significant is the lawyer who has no chance to win, nothing to lose, or who simply can gain an advantage by delay. In each of these cases, a jury trial is advantageous.

In a case in which the lawyer cannot fool a judge, he may well be able to fool a jury or one juror. If that juror is the "jury expert" or for some other reason is the most significant juror, a case can be won in front of the jury when it would have been lost before a judge. A jury is generally the best choice for a lawyer who has a bad case and must create a fiction in the courtroom. For the lawyer who has nothing to lose by litigation, a jury trial can be great fun. The lawyer hammers away and hopes the jury buys his position. The other lawyer must take his good or just case and sweat the jury's buying into his opponent's arguments or fictions and coming up with some sort of squirrelly decision. Juries often do squirrelly things.

Second only to intentionally misleading juries is taking inappropriate subjects before this early-American institution. Subjects that are too technical or too legally complex should not be tried before a jury. In these cases, the side that has less to explain or educate the jury about has a tremendous advantage.

Some of the cases before our courts are so technologically or legally complex that it takes technical and legal experts years to understand their many facets or the laws governing them. To expect jurors to understand these cases, after formal testimony and starched instructions from a judge, does not make sense. In reality they do not understand, and their decisions are a mixture of assumptions and guesses. That is a terrible way to run any institution.

When testimony and summation by the attorneys are completed in a trial, the judge reads the instructions (the law applicable to the case) to the jury. Prior to their deliberations the jurors are sworn to follow the law as read to them by the judge. Deliberations are supposed to be guided by the law. But what happens if the jury cannot understand the law? The obvious: there is often an incorrect decision that has the ring of finality about it—the jury has spoken.

At the insistence of opposing counsel, I recently tried a totally inappropriate case before a jury. The meaning of the law read to the jury had been battled over by four attorneys for almost two years. Neither the judge nor the attorneys were completely sure what it all meant. The case involved a lease-option contract, and the legal subjects included the statute of frauds, agency, oral contracts, implied agency, estoppel, eviction, breach of contract, specific performance, ejectment, written contracts, damages, punitive damages, and the relationships among them.

At the close of testimony, the eyes of the jurors glazed over as the judge spent thirty minutes reading these legal concepts in his monotone. His last words were, "For two hundred years we have agreed to live by the laws. If you do not follow the law in making your decision, it will be a miscarriage of justice." The sad reality is that the jury did not have the slightest understanding of what he said. I barely understood the instructions, and I have a legal education with over twenty years of courtroom experience. When the jury was deliberating, I told the judge, "They did not understand you." He looked at me and said, "If I had read those instructions to the Supreme Court of the United States they would not have understood them." The jury returned a verdict that was unclear; and, at this writing, we are still in litigation over it.

I contend that juries rarely understand the law when the instructions read to them are complex. They then make a decision based on thinking that is quite different from that of the actual law and the judicial officers in the courtroom. To try to undo what a confused or non-understanding jury has done costs American citizens billions of dollars each year.

The jury system is based on the premise that the judge will read the law to the jurors and that they will understand it. However, if they do not understand the instructions, the jury system fails. These instructions are compiled, studied, argued over, and presented to the judge by the attorneys. Frequently, neither judge nor attorneys can understand the subtleties of the instructions after research, deliberation, and argument. This failure to communicate is typical in complex civil cases, less frequent in simple criminal cases, but reverts back to typical in complex or showcase criminal trials.

The reading to jurors of instructions that they do not understand is a daily occurrence in American courtrooms. This process, in complex cases, degenerates to the point of silliness. The verdicts rendered are often inappropriate, which means the system is working poorly and doing unjust harm to the lives and families of millions of Americans. The victims of the inappropriate verdicts are understandably outraged and disgusted with the system. The process is time consuming and prohibitively expensive even when it does work. When it fails, which is regularly, the participants can be legally and financially devastated. We put up with these fictions because we have not understood how faulty the system can be.

Psychologists are now examining juror stress. When jurors are subjected to marathon show-business trials with copious amounts of complex information, it is not surprising that they are stressed. It is not surprising that jurors subjected to legal, sociological, and psychological theories propounded by expert witnesses day after day arrive at verdicts that perplex and stun their fellow citizens.

Jury service, a social event in early America, is a nightmare in technological America. Citizens want the concept of a jury trial. However, few want to serve, and low- to middle-income Americans find service an unacceptable financial burden. So many people avoid jury duty by not registering to vote that some states are turning to driver's-license registration for jurors.

Most of us like to think we have a right to trial by a jury of our peers. The jury-trial system evolved in the first place because commoners did not trust a system in which they were tried by nobility. We have come full circle. We are now tried by jurors who may be our technological, financial, or educational superiors. Even worse is being tried by jurors who have a substantially different cultural or racial background. Ask Black Americans.

We are maintaining a jury system that was appropriate to colonial agricultural America but inappropriate in modern technological America. It is just not working very well, and our citizens are suffering profoundly for our ignorance and unwillingness to address this problem adequately.

A Miscarriage of Justice

I had represented Dwayne since he was about fourteen years old for one juvenile crime after another. To Dwayne's credit, these were not violent crimes, but rather, petty theft, grand theft, larceny of a motor vehicle, and the like. Now, at eighteen, he was charged with his first adult crime, burglary, and the prosecuting attorney was going to put Dwayne away on this first one, if possible. A few hours in juvenile detention was the only time Dwayne had ever pulled. He had years of probation under his belt and so much counseling he knew the routines by heart. But that was over, if the prosecutor had anything to do with it, and he had a lot to do with it. He and the cops intended, using the popular basketball jargon, to slam dunk Dwayne.

Dwayne had been arrested one block away, jogging from the crime scene. The time was 2 A.M. He was dressed in appropriate burglar regalia: black shorts, black tee shirt, tennis shoes, and a dark knit hat covering his light blond hair.

With an alarm sounding and Dwayne jogging away from a crime scene, the police arrested him over vociferous protests and plunked him into the back of a patrol car. Dwayne knew these cops from previous engagements, so he criticized their parentage and kicked a couple of the windows out of the patrol car to show them he was unhappy. They thumped him a couple of times to show him they were unhappy, and he settled in for the ride to jail.

The police report said Dwayne had been apprehended fleeing from the scene of a burglary at a beer-distribution company. There were several persons involved, but the only one they could put their hands on was Dwayne. To enhance their case, they had recovered a beer can with Dwayne's fingerprints on it. No question about it, the prints were good. The lab had a match, and that match was Dwayne.

To make matters worse, the beer can had been found on the tailgate of a truck which had been broken open and from which beer had been stolen. Even worse than that, the truck was parked in the middle of the yard some fifty or sixty feet inside a chain-link fence.

Mom bailed Dwayne out of jail later that morning. Mom was a neat lady. She was blond, thirty-fiveish, attractive. Of her two sons, one was an average-looking boy two years Dwayne's junior who was an honest kid and an honor student. Then she had Dwayne. Dwayne was a handsome young man with an engaging personalty and a winning smile, and a quick but dishonest brain. Dwayne was her favorite. She was a long-suffering lady. She worked hard to support the two boys with no help from their father, who had bugged out years ago. She had been paying ten or fifteen dollars a week faithfully on

Dwayne's legal bills and was to spend the better part of two decades paying for his juvenile and young-adult crimes.

In any case, after obtaining discovery from the prosecution I realized we had one tough row to hoe. Dwayne had been arrested at 2 A.M. dressed like a burglar, running from a fresh crime scene, with no logical reason to be in the area, his fingerprints on a beer can inside the fence at the scene. After talking to the prosecutor, I saw the hoe-row grow longer and tougher. They too were familiar with Dwayne and his long juvenile record bringing only scoldings and slaps on the wrist: no deal. Dwayne could plead straight up to the charge and throw himself on the mercy of the court, or he could take his chances in front of a jury. There was not going to be much mercy from the court, so we were left with the jury: maybe we could fool them—the American trial lawyer's proud tradition.

We lawyers, members of bar associations with disciplinary and ethical rules, are forbidden to knowingly lie to juries or to judges, or to stand idly by while our clients or their witnesses lie with our knowledge. So we find ways around these rules, or we knowingly violate them—or lose our cases and starve to death.

Good trial lawyers have an easy way around the rules. Contrary to popular television fiction, we do not want, nor allow, our clients to tell us everything. In fact, we forbid it and will not listen. We tell our clients: you are not tried for what you did; you are tried by what the cops say you did. The police version ends up as varying degrees of truth and fiction. Truth is what they actually learn in their investigation, and the fiction is what they fill in to make their cases stick. To beat their fictions with truth is almost impossible even when the suspect is innocent, and he usually is not. So the best lawyers prepare themselves for a world-class lying contest called the American jury trial, and may the best-coached liars win.

The only statement Dwayne had made to the police was his explanation for being about at that early hour. He had been at a beach party with friends and was jogging home for health and exercise. The beer company was in a direct line from the beach to his home, though several miles away. They did not believe him, and neither did I, but that was Dwayne's story, and he was entitled to it. The major problem was the beer can with his fingerprints on it. I told him that he either explained the can away or he was going away. Dwayne was a smart guy; I had faith in his creative abilities.

At trial the prosecution and their witnesses were prohibited from making any mention of Dwayne's juvenile record in front of the jury. Combined with the jury system, this is a really dumb law, but it helps to fool them and keep America's crime rate high enough to maintain employment for even mediocre lawyers. To the jury, Dwayne was a young man with no prior record and, of course, the presumption of innocence.

The courtroom configuration was such that the defense table was on the left next to the jury box. It was a small courtroom, so the end of the defense table was within two feet of the jurors. We were so close to the jury that the prosecution table seemed almost remote, even in the small courtroom.

I placed Dwayne on my left, closest to the jury. I told him to make eye contact, smile, laugh at anything humorous, look innocent. I told him to fall in love with the jurors and make them fall in love with them, to cultivate with his eyes and demeanor anyone who appeared the slightest bit sympathetic. If the prosecution looked professional—I knew they would—and I looked a little lost, maybe they would think the defense was better than its lawyer. I did not care if they thought the defense lawyer was an idiot, as long as they said "not guilty."

The prosecution put on a straightforward trial. The police officers testified about the break-in and about apprehending

Dwayne running away from the scene. The laboratory technician brought the beer can and testified as to the match of fingerprints. They built a solid, air-tight case against Dwayne.

Dwayne sat through the testimony all smiles, spoke politely to the police as they trooped on and off the witness stand, and seemed to be enjoying the show. Dwayne even chuckled when the laboratory technician testified about the beer can.

The jury seemed perplexed. As the prosecution case grew tighter and tighter, Dwayne smiled wider and wider. Either he wanted to go to prison, or he had a reasonable explanation for all this damning testimony. The boy was good! Every iota of the acting ability of the accomplished sociopath was coming through. He was so much into the lies he intended to tell that he even believed them.

By this time he had told me his story, and it was my responsibility to defend him to the best of my ability, even if I did not believe him. I had no legal or ethical right to judge Dwayne. That was the job of the jury—a wonderful cop-out for the American trial lawyer. With this cop-out we can help keep America's most monstrous felons walking the streets, preying again on the population with a clear conscience. American trial lawyers are the one arm of the legal process that has a constitutional responsibility to do its ethical best to keep America's crime rate soaring. I am certain that is what the founding fathers had in mind (just like assault weapons in the hands of juvenile morons when the fathers wanted our people to be able to keep muskets to protect themselves from "the merciless Indian Savages"—T. Jefferson, Declaration of Independence.)

In any case, the prosecution rested, and it was time for the defense. There was only one witness, Dwayne. Dwayne confidently strode to the witness stand, proudly took the oath to tell the truth, then turned to smile at the jurors and make eye contact with each one of them. I was already proud of him.

He began by telling the jury that after high school (Dwayne had never graduated, but the prosecution never thought to go into that after hearing the rest of his testimony) he had worked a night job, so he became nocturnal. He was used to working or roaming at night and sleeping during the day; I knew this to be true because he committed his crimes at night. If he was not working, he stayed in shape by jogging to the beach at night. Had not the police testified they had seen him before, at night? They had. They had been trying to hint they had busted him before but were forbidden to do so by the law.

On this particular night he had been jogging his normal route, back from the beach, when he passed the beer-distribution compound. He saw activity in the compound, particularly around the back of one of the beer trucks. He stopped jogging, walked over, and looked through the chain-link fence. He saw three or four teenagers breaking into the back of a beer truck. Being a good citizen, he asked them what they were doing, which startled them. One of the teenagers, hoping to appease him, threw a beer can over the fence. It clunked a few feet from Dwayne, but since it was dark he did not know what it was, he walked over and picked it up. Seeing it was beer (he told the jury he did not drink), he threw the can back to the teenager, who placed it on the tailgate. He told this tale convincingly: so much for the prosecution fingerprints.

At about that time one of the teenagers set off an alarm and they all scattered. Dwayne, knowing he was in the wrong place at the wrong time, went about his business until the police stopped him. Of course Dwayne had tried to explain to the police, but they were being unreasonable and dead set on arresting somebody; he was convenient.

Why did he kick the windows out of the patrol car? Well, the officers had been very rough with him trying to get him to give up confederates he did not have. When he did not give them names he did not know, they tightened the cuffs to the point they were damaging nerves and cutting off the blood flow to his hands—all extremely painful. They then left him in the car to suffer. He kicked on the windows to get their attention. He showed the jury his still-injured wrists and the places where the cops had beaten on him. They had mistreated the hell out of an innocent guy, but he forgave them because he understood their mistake. They were just trying to do their jobs and protect the good citizens. Had he not smiled and spoken to those fine officers in the courtroom?

The jury swallowed this stuff right down to the end of their colons. They had before them a polite, soft-spoken young man, and the prosecution could not shake his story. Dwayne was a defense lawyer's dream. He looked the prosecution directly in the eyes and promptly answered every question. He was extremely polite and followed my instructions to the letter. The louder and more frustrated the prosecuting attorney became, the softer and more politely Dwayne answered the questions. By the time the prosecutor finished, Dwayne looked like the good guy and the prosecutor looked like the bad one.

The jury deliberated only a few minutes and came back with a not-guilty verdict. Dwayne, delighted, asked me if he should thank the jury. I was just tired and told him I did not care what he did. The prosecution was disgusted and the cops were outraged. While Dwayne was over shaking hands and hugging jurors—some of the ladies actually kissed him—I packed up and turned to look at his mother, who had been seated directly behind us during the trial. She looked at me with a quiet resignation and said: "God, what a miscarriage of justice."

"I know," I responded, and left the courtroom.

Several years and many offenses later, I asked Dwayne when the crimes would stop. He smiled his warm smile and said,

"When I'm dead."

Phil

Within the year I had an opportunity to "do" the same prosecutor again. Phil had been arrested for burglarizing an automobile dealership. More specifically, Phil had stolen a wheel from a new automobile.

Phil was a thirtyish male Caucasian who had held various employment—a family man. Phil was also a petty-thief-employee type character. He had been caught several times over the years but had never been "down" for any hard time. He was one of those people who plague business owners. While he works for a company, he is inside pilfering everything he can get his hands on. One story about Phil goes that he was stealing fifty-pound bags of the material industry throws on concrete floors to absorb oil and other spills. Over several years, after he had taken about twelve hundred pounds of the stuff, a neighbor asked him what he was going to do with it. He replied that he used it for kitty litter. The neighbor, surprised, did not know Phil owned a cat. He didn't, but he might own one some day.

In this particular case, Phil worked as a mechanic at an automobile dealership; he was a pretty good mechanic. Phil knocked off work at five on an early summer evening and went home. After dinner, about 7:30, Phil told his sweet wife he had to run an errand and drove back to the dealership, which had closed at 7:00.

It was still light out when he went to the front gate and tried his key. He was perplexed when it did not work. The dealership had changed all the locks the previous day to try to stem the hemorrhage of parts and equipment flowing through the gates after business hours. Only manager types had keys now. All employees were now forbidden to use the dealership equipment to work on their personal automobile projects because of the after-hours pilfering. This employee loss of a valuable privilege was courtesy of Phil. Phil checked all his keys, and when none worked, it dawned on him that maybe the dealership was noticing the losses. A little more cautious, he looked around for a security guard or anyone else who might be present. Discerning no one, he shouted several times. Still no one. He climbed back into his car and drove to the end of the dealership security fence. He walked along the fence to the back where the employees had a crawl-hole under the fence to go to a neighboring convenience store rather than walk or drive all the way around.

Phil crawled under the fence and walked to a new automobile in the middle of the service area. Unknown to him, he was being watched all the way. He pulled from his pocket a set of keys he had taken from the vehicle during the work day. He opened the trunk and removed a new wheel and tire, checked it over (there was still plenty of light), then slammed the trunk and returned to his car along the same route he had taken entering the compound. He drove home immediately, putting the stolen wheel in his carport.

From the time Phil first arrived at the dealership to try the key in the front gate lock, until the time he had driven away with the new wheel had taken between ten and fifteen minutes. He was home, maybe a mile away, drinking his third beer when the police arrived to arrest him for the burglary and take the wheel. This was maybe an hour and a half after he had returned from the dealership and well after dark.

The assistant manager had been on a trip across the state and had returned to the dealership after hours and shortly before Phil had arrived at the front gate. He was in his office when he heard Phil shouting. Rather than respond, he had watched Phil and telephoned the police to report the burglary. When they arrived, he gave them the complete scenario and a positive identification of Phil.

Things looked grim for Phil when the state would not deal and we were facing a jury with the stolen property in hand and a positive identification of the thief. I decided to take the oral statement of all the prosecution witnesses, a deposition, to see if I could find out what really happened, or a weakness in the state's case.

Phil claimed he had only borrowed the tire to see if it would fit a buggy he was building. In fact, he had borrowed a lot of things from the dealership. The dealership already knew that. Phil just omitted the part about forgetting to return the borrowed things.

I took the deposition of the assistant manager first. He went through the events pretty much as I have described them. He was sure of the identification; there was plenty of light out. Sure of that? Positive. When he finished, I took him back through the episode, asking him to give me the time and the time intervals between each step. He went back through and gave me a logical sequence and was sure of his steps. From Phil's shouting until he was at the end of the fence was a minute to a minute and a half. He had walked down the fence and was into the compound in another minute or so. He had spent only two or three minutes in the compound, no more than five minutes, and had returned along the same route. The whole burglary had taken place within a fifteen-minute time envelope.

I was particularly interested in the fourth dimension, time, during this period of my trial career. I looked at time carefully in each case. I was working on a theory. If I could control (or more correctly, pervert) the time sequence in a criminal trial, I could win—fool the jury—pretty much regardless of the rest of the facts of the case. Kick the case into the fourth dimension and force the prosecution to battle in the twilight zone. When had the assistant manager called the police? When Phil was returning to his vehicle along the fence perimeter. What happened then? The police came. What happened then? The assistant manager told them who had taken the tire and where he lived. The police already knew Phil and knew where he lived; they had been there before. What did the police do then? They left. The assistant manager went home. The assistant manager's testimony and story seemed simple and straightforward, nothing here.

Before I took the deposition of the officers, I reread their report. They received a "burglary-in-progress" code, sped to the scene, were told by the assistant manager the identity of the burglar, sped to the burglar's residence, and took him and the evidence into custody. Time of call: 2105 hours; time of arrest: 2120 hours. Officer cleared by 2200 hours. Whoa! That's well after dark and a long time after 7:30, 1930 hours.

I looked back at the report. The code was "burglary-in-progress." Either the officers went to dinner after the call and before they responded, or they had put the time on the report incorrectly. Yet it matched with what Phil told me about the time of the police arrival at his house. I checked the jail records; Phil had been in receiving at 2150 hours. The jailer's records were consistent with the officer's records and what Phil had told me about the time of the arrest, an hour and a half after he had returned home.

Phil did not deny going to the dealership and taking the wheel, and the time of his arrival was consistent with what the assistant manager said and daylight. The inconsistency was the "burglary-in-progress" code, the time the assistant manager had called the police—when Phil was returning to his automobile with the tire, and the time on the police and jail reports.

Something was wrong. The "burglary-in-progress" code had to be incorrect, so I took the officer's deposition.

"Yes, the burglary-in-progress code was correct." The "burglary-in-progress" call came over the radio at 2105 hours. Okay. What was the response time? Immediate. What did that mean? It was an emergency code; they rolled. How many miles away were they from the dealership? Miles? They were a block and a half from the dealership when they got the code. "Man, a burglary in progress, we called for backup and punched it. That engine almost yanked the frame out of the patrol car's body." He laughed. "We were at the dealership in fifteen seconds, give or take five seconds." It had to be the dispatcher.

I took the deposition of the dispatcher. Sure enough, telephone call came from the victim at 2105 hours, dispatched at 21:05:03 hours. Well, the dispatch logs were consistent; the dispatcher had not gone home to dinner between the assistant manager's call and the code to the patrol car.

Great! I was in the twilight zone. The assistant manager made a telephone call when Phil was returning along the fence, at least thirty seconds from his car. The dispatch is within three seconds, received at the speed of light, and the officers are fifteen seconds en route. They arrive on the scene over an hour after Phil had been gone from the premises, and the sun has long since been swallowed by the western horizon: a time warp.

I was excited at first, then puzzled. I checked and rechecked the testimony against the reports and what Phil told me. Any way it was examined, the time sequences did not correlate. I had a defense, but it could get away from me. If I knew why the times did not check out, maybe I could make the defense stick. I did not believe I could sell a jury on time warps.

I believed the assistant manager was lying about when he called the police. But why? Phil stuck to his story about borrowing the wheel. He said the assistant manager was not worried about the wheel, but probably thought about it for an hour or so, then decided he would turn Phil in to the police to get him fired. It was a good explanation and might fly.

I asked around and came across one of my clients who knew the assistant manager and his habits. What he told me answered my questions. It seemed the assistant manager went across state to an automobile auction once a week. He always took the same secretary, and on return they enjoyed the casting couch in his office. Since his wife expected him to be late and the place was closed, he had been getting away with it for years.

If he called the police right away, he would have either had to interrupt his tryst or risk his girlfriend's name being beside his on the police report, as a witness. If his wife happened to attend the trial and saw his secretary as an after-hours co-witness, well, she was not that stupid.

So he waited until the deed was finished and girlfriend was away before he called in the burglary. But why report a burglary in progress? No choice. No jury would believe someone waits an hour, under these circumstances, to report a crime if he believes what he is observing is a crime.

During jury selection I asked the normal general questions, then sandwiched solidly one concept among the questions directed toward this type of case. I got from each juror an implied promise he or she would never convict a person if he or she believed the key witness against him was lying. It seemed a logical, straightforward question that went right over the prosecution's head. They had neither the time nor inclination to study the time sequences as closely as I, and had no idea where the defense was going.

As in Dwayne's case, the prosecution put on a good, solid case. The assistant manager told his story, and the police told their story. The key in this case was going to be cross examination; and that, contrary to popular myth, is super dangerous. It is not fun like on television; it's difficult to do well; most lawyers do it poorly, and it makes my hands sweat.

Most lawyers lose cases on cross; they do not win them on cross. It is hard to teach because so much is instinct or intuition. A few rules: Do not ask questions when you do not know the answers. Never repeat the direct examination or let the witness say damaging things twice; it is bad enough that the jury heard it the first time. And the most important rule: don't cross examine. Most lawyers just gotta do it because that's what happens on television. If the witness did not hurt your case, keep your mouth shut.

In this case, my thieving client's future hung not only on a good cross examination, but on my breaking all the rules. I amateurishly took the prosecution witnesses back through the direct. The only thing I did was to keep asking over and over, are you sure about that? More importantly, are you sure about the time? I nailed time down and renailed it until the prosecution objected. I slid in daylight and darkness as cleverly as possible. This was a good prosecutor used to dealing with amateur lawyers who do this sort of repetition of direct all the time. He was disgusted with the routine and slept through most of it, until it became so tedious he had to object.

By the time I finished, two very important things had happened. The prosecutor had no idea, in our little game of deception, where I was going, and the jury knew a lot they did not know they knew. They knew the times and the time sequences of each event in detail, but not in order. By the time the prosecution rested, this case was in the bag if I could get past my witness without disaster.

Phil was not the clever sociopath that Dwayne was. He was surely a sociopath but slower and prone to make mistakes. He had to get on the stand and say he borrowed the tire; and remember the cops had taken it from his carport. He had to do exactly what I told him: KISS, Keep It Simple, Stupid. I took him through the crime and refastened the time sequences in the jurors' minds; then I sat down. Phil had no idea what our defense was other than that he was going to return the wheel. If he stuck to that simple story on cross, we might get out of here. When the prosecutor stood up to cross, I held my breath. This guy was good. He was smart, and he knew Phil was a petty thief. KISS, again. I had told Phil to keep his answers short, admit good things, deny bad things, and not try to explain anything. If you get into trouble, just say you do not understand and I will try to rehabilitate you on redirect.

The prosecutor did exactly what I thought he would. He figured he had this case won. He asked but one or two innocuous questions and sat down. I could have kissed him. More importantly, I could have kissed my crook: no damage! Now, if I could put summation together without doing something stupid, we were outta here.

In this court, in a criminal case, the defendant gets last argument if he puts on no witnesses or only the defendant as a witness. In other words, I get a brief opening, prosecution gets rebuttal, I get last word. The trick, I had to lay out my time sequence but not tip the concept until I put it together after the prosecution was finished.

I opened summation by saying I would prove only one point: that the prosecution's main witness was lying. Then I went through the testimony, out of sequence, but stating the times. I mentioned everything, put all the parts of the picture together, but did not collate them. I closed this part of the opening by emphasizing that the assistant manager was lying, but they still could not see it. The prosecution did a low-key competent summation and put together the crime scenario, scoffing at the lying concept. When he was finished, I put it together for the jury, and the prosecutor had to sit in stunned silence.

The alleged crime took place, in broad daylight, seven thirtyish. No question, the jury understood that. The assistant manager called the cops when Phil was walking along the fence to his car with the stolen wheel. No question about it. Still daylight. I drew a picture on the blackboard. The police were dispatched immediately. Yes, the jury understood that. "Burglary in progress," they blew the pistons out of the patrol car. Yes, the cops said that. A block and a half, they are on the crime scene in fifteen seconds. True, the jury was right with me. Now the curve. The police arrive on the crime scene after dark, and the defendant has been gone for an hour and a half. I paused and looked at their eyes, then looked at the slumbering prosecutor.

I could see the adrenalin hit: panic! all is lost! too late! no way to rebut. Fear, denial, anger, and acceptance; that 140-plus IQ processed the death-defeat sequence in a microsecond.

I looked back at the jurors: bingo, I got one. Juror number three, the engineer, smiled; the lightbulb between his ears was ignited. The others were struggling, I nudged, I said it again: bingo, I got two more. Time to chill out.

I am nice now. I philosophize. I don't know why the assistant manager is lying about Phil, but I know he is lying, and you know it too. You, the jury, can send Phil to prison, but you have to do it over the lies of the prosecution's key witness. I go into all the good stuff about sleeping at night after sending a man to prison, knowing the key witness is lying. They are shaking their heads, no; and the prosecution gets no rebuttal. Time to shut up and sit down.

While the judge reads the instructions to the jury, Phil asks me what I think. He does not have a clue. I do something I never, never do. I never predict what a jury will do. I lean over and tell him to relax; when the judge finishes this nonsense, the jury will leave for a few minutes, and when they come back, he can go home. They were out for ten minutes longer than I thought: the ladies had to go to the bathroom.

Now what is the point of these two little stories? The point is: a clever lawyer, me, fooled two juries of very nice American citizens, and let two crooks free. Both of them subsequently went to prison for later criminal offenses.

If this took place in isolation, it would be okay. This is a big, powerful country with the ability to absorb an abundance of insult from its institutions and the officers who function in them. But these cases are not in isolation. This country has a host of clever, really smart criminal-trial lawyers. These little legal operas are going on in thousands of courtrooms every day, all day long, in this country. They keep our streets flooded with criminals and we, as a nation, wonder what is wrong.

What is wrong is that our criminal-justice system is a horse-and-buggy institution based on outdated premises. The idea that we can make these lying contests into truth and justice is fallacious. A trial system whose foundation is deception, illusion, and even dishonesty and showmanship is doomed to failure. And, as I have pointed out, it is failing. It is indefensible that a great democracy, based on noble principles, defends those principles with lawyers who are lauded and employed for their cleverness in deceiving the triers of fact, the judges and jurors. If we maintain this system, we will find it very difficult to control our criminals without instituting a police state and defeating the principles the system is charged to protect.

Notes

1. Callins v. Collins.

CHAPTER III

THE UNAFFORDABLE SYSTEM

The American legal system is too complex and too expensive. Because of its complexity it has evolved into a system that only the wealthy can fully employ. Occasionally even lawyers need lawyers to help them with its complexities. This illustrates why very few citizens have the knowledge to represent themselves. The middle-income or low-income citizen cannot afford to utilize the legal system in day-to-day affairs; the economics of the practice of law forbids it.

The lawyer must pay rent, electricity, secretarial salaries, insurance, bills for legal books, office supplies, transportation, and taxes before he or she can take home a paycheck. I am familiar with a two-lawyer or three-lawyer office where the overhead ranges from $125,000 to $160,000 per year. Each attorney must contribute $1000 or more each week. If a lawyer can bill five hours per day, five days per week, at $100 an hour, and can actually collect all the fees, the gross is $2500 a week, and the lawyer's income looks like $50,000-$60,000 per year. The problem is, it never works out that way.

Five hours per day is a lot of time to be mentally engaged, and few lawyers do top-quality work five hours per day, day after day. Even the lawyers who do it must subtract from possible billable days vacation, holidays, sick days, and days unavoidably wasted. When these hours are subtracted, along with the worst hemorrhage, legal fees that are not collectable, up to one third in some cases, one hundred dollars an hour is a living at best and poverty wages at worst. The lawyer has three choices: work himself to death (it happens a lot), raise the hourly rates, or fudge on the hours worked. The ones who burn out or work themselves to death disappear; most others raise their rates. Many big law firms insist that their junior associates bill forty and sometimes sixty hours per week. These associates rarely do sixty hours of real work each week, so they are billing with a heavy pencil. However, this book is not about praising or criticizing lawyers, their work, or their billing practices, or even the profession in general. Rather it is discussing the effect of their necessarily high rates on the legal system. To make a decent living, lawyers have to apply these rates to complex and time-consuming lawsuits. This in turn renders the American legal system unaffordable to low-income and middle-income working persons.

The standard of proof is the same for a $3000 lawsuit as it is for a $300,000 lawsuit. The number of legal hours required to prove a $3000 lawsuit may be the same as for the $300,000 lawsuit, and if the facts are more convoluted in the $3000 lawsuit, the legal hours may be more. If it takes $30,000 to prove a $300,000 lawsuit and $30,000 to prove the $3000 lawsuit, the victor in the $3000 lawsuit is a loser by a factor of ten.

The large corporation can almost always beat the working person out of a few thousand dollars in any controversy. The contracts of large corporations are too wordy and complex for persons not legally trained to understand or interpret adequately. The cost of a lawyer to fight the big corporation is too much for the little people, and the big outfits know it. Therefore, in a money controversy, the little person must rely on the good will of the big corporation, spend precious resources to crusade against it, petition a regulatory agency, or take his losses and walk away because the American legal system is too expensive.

This failure of the American legal system is tacitly recognized by both business and government. Government has created a maze of regulatory agencies to assist the consumer. These agencies are a costly, complex mess. Business has created dispute-resolution procedures to protect itself from having to bother with the regulatory agencies. Neither business nor government has thought to change the legal system so that it will work for all our citizens and eliminate the bulk of these costly agencies.

Fortunately, most middle-income citizens never become involved in complex civil or criminal litigation. John and Jane Doe Citizen have but a distant view of the legal system. They studied civics in middle school, and the rest of their legal education has come from the media. They tend to believe that lawsuits are like what they see in the movies or on television. Of course, television lawsuits never discuss the prohibitive costs and legal fees. From the news media, Mr. and Mrs. Citizen see only the tip of the iceberg.

Being involved in a dispute with a neighbor, a product dispute, or a minor criminal or traffic problem can bring the reality of the legal system crashing down on the low-income or middle-income family. A $15,000 problem may take one or two years to wind through the court system, causing the attorney to expend an average of one or two hours per week throughout this time. Legal fees at $150 per hour or $300 per week or $15,600 per year for the duration become more than significant to a family that is barely making it without legal problems.

Banks, insurance companies, product manufacturers, and wealthy folks know they can financially beat the middle-income and low- income citizen to death by using the legal system's delay-rich procedures to incur high legal costs. Unscrupulous businesses knowingly use the legal system to beat the lower-income citizen into financial submission. This amounts to a legal system based on the good will of financial superiors. It is common in litigation for one party to tell the other, "I can outspend you!"

When the citizen hears the businessperson say, "If you don't like it, sue me," he soon recognizes that his choice is to take the loss or to sacrifice vacations, new cars, or education for his children to fight for what may well amount to a principle. Most people, if they have knowledgable legal advice, just take the loss and walk away.

Until a middle-income citizen becomes involved in one of these expensive lawsuits, he has no idea how expensive the legal system is and how poorly it works. The wealthy citizen does not like it either, but the wealthy citizen has a tremendous advantage over a lower-income American. Conversely, this is not a rich-versus-poor issue. When a trial lawyer looks to sue someone, he looks for the deep pocket. To paraphrase Ralph Nader, our legal system is unsafe at any income level.

Once bitten, the middle-income citizen learns to avoid the legal system if possible. The low-income citizen, without pro bono services or some other assistance, is financially out of the game and cannot afford to use the legal system. What we have is a legal system that most of our citizens cannot afford to use. A legal system should not be too expensive to use, and it does not need to be this expensive. We need to--and can--change the system so that all our citizens can afford to use it.

Diane

Diane heard those terrible words: "I have more money than you; I'll out-spend you in court and on legal fees; I'll break you; you can't win." Those angry words initiated a long, expensive legal battle over what the builder described as a "sun-drenched hideaway."

A middle-income public-school teacher, Diane was scouting the residential neighborhoods of her small Sunbelt city looking for just the right home when she spotted a charming sculpture in wood. The small, two-story house was situated on an ample lot in a secure neighborhood and snuggled in amongst the pine trees. With two small outbuildings, one a garage, and a wide screen-enclosed side porch, it would more than suit her needs.

On investigation, Diane learned the house could be purchased from the owner-builder within her budget if she struggled and did without. The house was new, having been recently completed by the owner-builder, himself the occupant. In fact, the owner-builder was working on another house and, if Diane purchased the house, would request a lease back for a few months.

If anything, the owner-builder was not spartan in his praise for the house, its structure, and the care and quality of his craftsmanship. He described the house as a handcrafted home, the design his own and each nail personally driven with care if not affection. He knew every nook and cranny of the house; he befriended Diane and assured her that he, the builder himself, would be living right down the street in his new handcrafted home and would come running should she ever experience a problem. After all, the house was beautiful; and after carefully looking over the house, she found no visible flaws. Learning that it had passed all county inspections, she was sold. He did not tell her he was an unlicensed builder--which seemed to make little difference, when the builder knew the right people.

After purchase and during the lease-back to the builder,

the doors began to stick, and Diane brought the problem to the attention of the builder, who assured her all was well: wooden doors always did that in these humid climes. The builder shaved the doors, and several months later Diane moved in and even served the builder and his lovely wife a Thanksgiving dinner. All was well except that those pesky doors were reacting to the humidity again and sticking. The builder sent a fellow over to reshave the doors, and it worked for a while.

Over the next year, all the doors and windows caught the humidity disease. In fact, the entire house seemed to catch the humidity disease as some floors developed an interesting slant and a scenic waviness developed from the kitchen through and into the living room. Diane called upon her builder, now a neighbor, and requested that he take a hard look at this situation. Since he had her money and was busy building more "sun-drenched hideaways" just like Diane's, he had no time to keep fooling with her. He angrily told her he did not know what could possibly be wrong with so fine a house and she should consult an engineer.

A cursory examination by the engineer--he did not do an intrusive inspection at this time--found the house to be differentially settling with subsequent wracking of the doors and windows. This could be caused by a lot of things having to do with the foundation. It could be some unknown soil condition, improperly compacted natural soil, some sort of liquidizing of the soil, insufficient piles, beams, or footers, or any combination thereof. In any case, the solution was to discover why, stabilize the soil or foundation, jack the house back into position, and repair the interior cracking of walls and the other problems that had ensued.

Diane was financially tapped out. She could hardly afford the engineer's inspection, so she went back to the builder with the engineer's preliminary report. The builder agreed to meet with Diane and the engineer. The negotiations were brief: it was not his fault; he could and would do nothing about it; caveat emptor; and you can sue or do anything else you want. "I'll beat you, I have more money than you do, I'll out-spend you on court and legal fees, I'll break you." With those glowing words ringing in her ears, Diane started lawyer shopping.

"Yes, if he can out-spend you, he will break you," I told her; and that was the good news. I am very up front with my clients about the failing American trial system and even a little sarcastic. Litigation of this sort is prohibitively expensive, with long court delays, discovery, motions, and costly expert fees and studies. We can probably win, but the builder will hide his assets and lie about them. I told her she would spend years in court, mortgage her future, and the person who cheated her would walk away having paid little or nothing, even if she won. I told her that this is not the movies or television. This is the real American legal system. It is too expensive for middle income citizens.

I outlined an alternative approach. She could take her complaints to the county building officials and try to use the county resources and attorneys to lean on the builder. I knew the county had good, strict building codes as twenty years previous I had written the ordinances incorporating the various southern standard building codes. I cautioned her that they were bureaucrats, who might consider her a nuisance and not be very helpful at all. In any case, going to the officials probably would not hurt other than a delay, and it could save her a fortune in legal fees. Boy, was I wrong! They did not just consider her a nuisance; they became her adversary and the champion of the unlicensed builder who had caused all the problems in the first place.

The county's bureaucratic dog-and-pony show began innocently enough. With great flourish and fanfare, the code-enforcement officials took out the approved plans, talked to Diane and her engineer and even her lawyer, me. They assured us they would jump on this problem, find the culprit, and Diane would have her house fixed or they would have somebody's head.

They called in the builder and the design professional. "The design professional?" We asked. We did not know there was a design professional. The builder had said the house was his design. In fact, when a popular southern magazine had featured this house, the builder was listed as the designer and was selling plans through the magazine.

The design professional, an architect, was another duck to shoot at. In the American legal system it is wise to shoot at all the ducks and see how many you hit. We watched, over the next several months, the bureaucratic duck-shooting machinations as they went after the design professional.

We came to understand what had taken place. The builder had hired an architect to draw a set of plans to his specifications, which were little more than sophisticated sketches. There was little detail on the plans; what was there was pretty good, but there were some questionable values that left much to interpretation. But the plans were good enough for an experienced builder to follow and certainly adequate to build a good house if the codes were followed.

The county told us the builder had agreed to repair the house if the design professional would do the repair drawings. The question became the extent of repair the county would force on the builder, the cost, and the sharing of cost between the builder and the architect. The architect did not believe this mess was his fault, and neither did Diane's engineer, but the architect was cooperative and worked with her engineer toward a solution.

After a rough drawing was completed that would relieve the differential settlement problem, we negotiated with the builder through the county. Offers, rejections, and discussions dragged on while the builder went after the design professional through the state professional regulatory authorities. What we did not know at the time was that the county bureaucrats were not playing the game straight. Every confidential discussion we had with the building officials was immediately relayed by those same officials to the unlicensed builder on the job site where he was building that next "sun-drenched hideaway."

We accepted several different cost-sharing proposals, and Diane actually signed one of the drawings. The builder balked. This process dragged on for over a year. The county officials feigned wringing their hands over the builder's lack of cooperation but would not play all their cards. I had identified a host of crimes--each code violation was a crime--and there was a possible felony involved. The county officials promised they would take the matter to the prosecutor if I outlined the crimes. They had the outline within hours. They delayed and delayed as a year slipped away.

By this time we were getting enough feedback to understand that the bureaucrats were not going to help Diane; in fact, they were solidly in the unlicensed builder's corner. Enough! We went to the county manager. With solemn promises, he assured us this man would build no more in his county if he did not fix the house. The builder would be prosecuted; he would be stomped. We did not need to go to the commissioners.

Sure enough, the officials asked the prosecutor to proceed, and the builder was wracked with a fifty-dollar fine as the statute of limitations ran on the rest of the crimes. We went to the commission. They were outraged when we outlined our problem and told them what their staff had been doing. They, in no uncertain terms, directed the bureaucrats to straighten this matter out regardless of whose head had to roll.

The bureaucrats responded. They ordered a study of the house by an out-of-town engineering firm. What the engineering firm's marching orders were we never did find out, but we suspected they were directed to go after the design professional. They spent over $20,000 of taxpayers' money studying Diane's house and came up with a fairly balanced report albeit inadequate in scope. They had performed no intrusive inspection. They found both design problems and construction problems. The design professional had been absolved of fault by the state board by this time. What the report did tell us was that Diane's house was in a lot worse shape than even we suspected.

By this time the builder knew the officials would do nothing to him, so he became totally uncooperative. The county officials would not force the builder, and were rapidly losing any leverage they might have had over him. We went back to the commission. The county manager had become uncooperative with us; he seemed to view Diane as the enemy, not the victim. He was a waste of time.

The Commission was again outraged and again ordered its bureaucrats to solve the problem. The bureaucrats responded by taking the builder before a code-enforcement board, cutting a deal with him, and letting him off the hook. He had to place $7,000 in escrow, and he was relieved of responsibility. From their own report, they now knew it would take tens of thousands of dollars to fix the house.

An election came, and the outraged commissioners who understood the problem were gone. The bureaucrats had stalled enough to protect their unlicensed builder who had violated virtually the entire ordinance book. What hold the builder had over the officials or why they acted as they did, we never did find out. We sued.

The reason we had spent over a year with the bureaucrats was the prohibitive expense of litigation in the American legal system. But we had gained one advantage: we had a $20,000 engineering report on Diane's house paid for by the taxpayers. We needed the expertise to prove our case in the legal system, and it had always been too expensive for Diane to purchase on her own.

To cut down on the anticipated expensive motion practice that accompanies most litigation, we flew across the state and copied the pleadings from a case decided by the Supreme Court that set the precedent for our issues. When the opposing attorney materialized, we told him, do not waste time and money; we copied the pleadings and here is the case cite; he took the advice. That is not to say the litigation was not slow and expensive; it was. It consumed most of the next year, push as we might, and it became very adversarial.

As is my wont, I tried to get the opposing attorney and his clients to listen and settle at a reasonable cost. I told them they could not win. That is a brave or foolish thing for a lawyer to say in this system, but we had the law on our side, and we had the facts, engineers, and reports. The opposition took the traditional adversarial stance. They would not even listen. I was terrified of a jury. With all the technical data and knowledge that the county officials would testify to protect the unlicensed builder, they might do anything. We had an intelligent, responsible judge, so I wanted to try the case before the judge. After some maneuvering, I managed to talk the opposing attorney out of a jury trial, and we avoided it.

At trial I called the builder. He admitted that he built the house, that he was an experienced builder who knew what he was doing. He denied there was much wrong with the house--a few little problems that could be inexpensively repaired.

I called a neighbor who had been told by the builder, "I build 'em cheap to sell 'em dear." Then I called our contractor and our engineer, who had completed several intrusive investigations. They testified the house had a negative economic value. It would be cheaper to tear it down and replace it.

The house was settling because the spans on the beams were too long and the piers themselves were settling. What the builder had done was to dig some holes too deep, then backfill without compacting the soil. Some piers were on compacted soil; some were not. The weight of the house was compacting the soil. The house was settling differentially, twisting the walls and wracking the windows and doors.

The nail pattern on the walls was inadequate; there were no fire stops in the walls. There were no ground-fault interruptors in the electrical system; there was no roof access and not even a roof diaphragm. What the builder had done was to nail galvanized steel roofing directly to the roof trusses without plywood under the steel and then not bother to use but a few hurricane clips. And this was just the beginning. There were dozens and dozens of small violations and hazards everywhere we looked. Stairs incorrect, no bird's mouth on the porches, septic system wrong, setbacks incorrect, and even an unpermitted structure on the property.

This house was a dangerous firetrap. The deficiencies were systematic and ubiquitous. These were not oversights. This was systematic cheap construction to save money, and it was all hidden from any reasonable inspection a home purchaser might be advised to contract. The house was beautiful, a sculpture in wood, as the engineer testified; and it was going to fall down sooner or later. Even the opposition's engineer admitted the house was in danger of falling down.

The judge visited the house and listened as both sides pointed out deficiencies and argued about them. At the conclusion of the trial, he awarded damages of $126,000.

Of course the builder appealed; of course the county would not give Diane the $7,000 in escrow without another fight and without strings attached. Of course the builder divested himself of all visible assets so that Diane could find no money for compensation. The builder testified to one of the old saws: he had gone to Atlantic City and gambled his money away in one night. "Sorry, I'm broke." As I had told her in the beginning, she won at great expense, and the person who cheated her paid little or nothing. A great legal system.

What was the cost of this exercise in the American legal system? Over $30,000 to Diane in attorney fees, and I did not even bill a substantial amount of my time. Almost $10,000 in expert fees. The opposition had to be as much or more. This case consumed over three years; it broke both parties; and no one was compensated but the attorneys. It could have been much worse. I was cost conscious and pushing hard all the time. Remember we obtained a $20,000 report on the taxpayers' nickel. If we had had to pay for all the engineering, the total of legal fees and expert fees would have been close to the value of the house.

If this case were atypical, it would be excusable, but it is not. Diane's case is not unusual at all. The cost of the litigation is frequently more than the subject of the suit. This is the norm in America's trial system, not the exception. As the society has grown more technologically sophisticated, litigation has grown more complex and expensive. In colonial America five dollars might have been worth the lawsuit. In technological America, $5,000 is not worth the lawsuit, almost never. In this case $100,000 was not worth the lawsuit.

Dishonest builders know the American legal system is neither quick enough nor cheap enough for the people they cheat to touch them. The shoddy building in South Florida contributed much to the destruction of hurricane Andrew for which the victims and the taxpayers suffered. The legal system was not adequate to protect those home purchasers then and is not adequate now.

As many have come to understand, the American trial system is almost useless for amounts of money other than small claims or megadollars. Why maintain a trial system that is too costly to use? We need to change our trial system. This system cannot be repaired; it should be replaced.

CHAPTER IV

BUSINESS

Business litigation in the adversarial jury-trial system is the most expensive and complex litigation in America. An indirect and unnecessary taxation imposed on American businesses is the cost of legal services fueled by a growing number of complex and protracted lawsuits. To be in business today too frequently requires suing to collect money or occasionally being sued over nonsense, with little protection from abuses. Part of every business's profit finds its way into the lawyer's pocket. An even larger amount of business profit is abandoned by small businesses because, as happens for middle-income citizens, it is too expensive to use the legal system for collection. The American legal system poorly serves the honest business community.

In the business world it is the small-business proprietor, like low-income and middle-income persons, who is taking the biggest hit from our adversarial legal system. The "mom-and-pop" business that pays its bills and makes an adequate income for one family can ill afford to become involved in a major lawsuit when it must pay legal fees of $150 an hour or more. Yet this is what happens every day across America.

The small businessman who has never been forced into

complex litigation has, like many citizens, little understanding of the expense and time involved. Those who are forced to tread this path are at first shocked, then, after one tough lawsuit, are wont to avoid litigation at virtually any cost.

Unfair and expensive to a business are the people who will litigate because they have nothing to lose. It is very dangerous to face a desperate person with a knife or a gun. A person with nothing to lose and a weapon is very likely to use that weapon. Litigation's dangerous equivalent is the business person who has nothing to lose by protracted litigation. As an example, a tenant or mortgagor retains possession of property by legal delay after legal delay while the landlord or mortgagee attempts to regain possession. The litigant uses the property or even collects rents, makes no payment, performs no maintenance, and allows the property to deteriorate during the lawsuit. Varying themes on this scenario abound throughout the business world. In many cases, there is no reasonable mechanism to obtain a timely remedy for the injured party.

In the home-construction industry, sub-contractors are especially vulnerable to being caught in litigation to recover a few thousand dollars when the developer and the contractor are struggling over millions. Another chronic problem is the owner or developer who never intends in the first place to pay the last draw to the sub-contractor or laborer. The court-wise owner or contractor knows the expense of litigation and knows the sub-contractor or laborer can ill afford to hire a lawyer to litigate over two or three thousand dollars.

This is especially so when the sub-contractor knows the contractor or owner is going to lie about the quality of work or other putative problems. All too frequently the sub-contractor or laborer walks away from some or all of his profit rather than pay attorney fees that would probably be more than the profits for which he is suing.

There are lien laws to protect the little guy, but they are too complex and too strict. It is difficult for lawyers to follow the lien laws without stepping into legal traps, yet the lawmakers expect the little guys to follow them. This same general pattern strikes small business after small business. In the adversarial jury system, the little guy gets hurt. For the small-business owner, we have not met the Constitutional promise of equal protection of the laws.

Fortunately, most big businesses, although at great expense, can take care of themselves in the courtroom. Large industries have in-house counsel and are covered by insurance companies who have an army of lawyers on retainer throughout the country. Big business has the money to survive sustained litigation and to hire the best adversaries.

Nevertheless, product-liability suits are needlessly destroying businesses and in some cases crippling whole industries. Even worse is the stifling of innovation to the extent that the public never sees new or improved products. When lawsuits remove dangerous products from the market or correct dangerous products, they are socially invaluable. On the other hand, product-liability lawsuits that stifle research or delay or arrest the introduction of new products are socially destructive. There are too few of the former and too many of the latter.

The added costs to production because of lawsuits, the stifling of innovation, and fear of introducing new products decrease American ability to compete in world markets. Our inefficient adversarial legal system has to be a factor in our trade deficit.

As an example, in the 1980's product-liability lawsuits almost destroyed the production of small general-aviation airplanes in the United States. By the end of the decade, more small airplanes were being built in garages and home workshops in America than in our factories. General aviation reverted to a cottage industry. One of the main reasons, if not the primary one, for the loss of this industry was the product-liability lawsuit.

An airplane is a high-tech machine, with thousands of parts; the failure of any one may cause an accident or great monetary loss. A lay jury is asked to decide high-tech cases when it has absolutely no ability to do so. Lawyers defending aviation industries have found it almost impossible to educate lay juries about aviation concepts during emotion-filled trials. To explain the necessary technology to the jurors, the lawyers hire experts who make charts, draw diagrams, make movies, and manufacture a host of other audio and visual displays. The best and often richest producer in this show-business affair wins millions of dollars and all too frequently hundreds of millions. Plaintiff lawyers drag out pictures of dead bodies for lay juries, while aviation-defense lawyers cannot drag out emotion-filled photos of a dying industry. A very personal tragedy for millions of Americans is the doctor they cannot afford to see and the drugs they cannot afford to buy. Doctors pay such outrageous premiums for malpractice insurance that they must keep raising their fees and perfect an assembly-line practice to make a decent living. Drugs manufactured for pennies cost tens of dollars to cover the litigation losses from the few that occasionally cause catastrophic side effects. Worse, some needed drugs are not placed on the market because of the fear of litigation. In short, our legal system is indirectly killing a lot of citizens because of their inability to pay for litigation-inflated medical care.

The next major industry threatened by the adversarial jury system is the tobacco industry. Unless big tobacco obtains legislative protection or understands the futility of attempting to defend itself in our dysfunctinal court system rather than helping to scrap this system in favor of a new one, most American cigarettes will by manufactured by small companies in a few years. The giants will have moved offshore or will be industrial passenger pigeons.

It is easier to delay and frustrate in the adversarial jury system than it is to accomplish a positive goal. The adversarial system emphasizes and rewards the negative rather than the positive. In the business world, the legal system is a safe haven for the crooked business person, the cheat, the liar, and the thief. A crooked business person can take a dishonest position, then lie with impunity in the courtroom. It is almost impossible to obtain a prosecution for perjury in business litigation. The business person who is willing to lie in a courtroom has a tremendous advantage. Prosecutors are in the rape and murder business, so there is little prosecution of white-collar crime and almost none for perjury. The prudent crook should "go business." With the aid of the American legal system, it is a lot safer and more profitable to steal the entire store than it is to rob it, and the successful crook may become citizen of the year.

The other side of the coin is to use this expensive system to litigate the small-business person to financial exhaustion. When the rich man's toy breaks, he can sue the small-repair or parts producer to fix his million-dollar machine. If the part is high-tech and the damages are in the hundreds of thousands, it is worth a shot for the rich guy to gamble twenty thousand for attorneys and experts to force the little guy to pay something or face financial ruin from the cost of litigation regardless of fault. Even if the little guy wins, the attorney fees he has had to pay may have financially destroyed him. Most people do not realize that, in most cases, the loser does not have to pay the winner's legal fees. Pyrrhic victories are common in the adversarial jury system. Big business, insurance companies, banks and just plain rich folks can and do use this expensive system to browbeat the small-business person into legal submission.

Many movements are afoot to limit liability in various industries. The aviation industry finally persuaded Congress to pass legislation limiting its liability, but the most successful industry has been the insurance industry. In Florida courts, the jury is not allowed to hear that the defendant in an automobile accident case has insurance. In every other trial, the real party in interest is clearly identified in a lawsuit. This has been of tremendous benefit to the insurance industry and terribly damaging to accident victims. Every industry under stress from product-liability suits is searching for legislative protection. These actions are piecemeal, patch-up solutions that are not solving the nationwide problem and never will solve it. It is time to identify and address the real problem facing American business in the legal world. The problem is not American industry, and it is not the legal profession. The problem is the American adversarial jury legal system itself and the way it operates.

Think of the anomaly of this whole silly business. American industries and business are forced to seek help from our legislative bodies in order to protect themselves from our dysfunctional courts.

When it is financially advantageous for a business entity to delay, the jury system is made to order. That is not the way to run a society and certainly not the way to run an economy. American business persons should welcome a fundamental change in our antiquated legal system as we continue our advance toward the Twenty-first Century and an ever more sophisticated economic system.

Contractor

Roy met with no little success in the construction business as a big frog in a little pond. As a single-family home builder who had worked his way into commercial construction, he provided a good product for the dollar. After raising his family and putting aside a nest egg, he felt it was time to leave the snow and work in the sun.

Re-establishing himself in the Sunbelt, he continued good construction for an honest profit. Roy was also physically a little closer to high-rise construction, the big-money casino. He watched with envy those who jumped into the big-money stakes and walked away millionaires. Among fellow contractors and subcontractors he talked the big game and listened with eager ears for the offer that would lead to an affluent retirement.

When he was big enough, and hungry enough, and ripe enough, the big offer came. He was offered a $12,000,000 contract on a one-year building-construction project. Roy's draw was to be roughly $1,000,000 per month with ten percent retainage; completion within the scheduled year would yield him, with a bonus, a total profit of considerably over a million dollars.

Roy invested his own money and jumped in with all four feet. He came out of the first month ahead of schedule, over quality, and under budget. He received his first $900,000 draw from the project manager on time, accompanied by a big, loud "attaboy." And so the project went month after month.

At the end of the ninth month with the project seventy-five percent completed, Roy bounced into the project manager's office to collect his $900,000 draw and was met with a grim-faced manager. The manager handed Roy a check for $500,000, $400,000 short of the expected draw. The check was accompanied by a long list of deficiencies and complaints about his work prepared by the project's architect. Roy made a brief protest but was curtly told to correct the deficiencies for the balance of his draw.

Roy returned to his construction trailer confused and heartsick but was much relieved when he studied the deficiency list. For the most part these were nothing but normal punch-list items that should and would be completed at the end of the job, plus a few major items that should have been scheduled later in the job but had been put in prematurely by the architect. There was nothing on the list that could not be readily explained, and a brief meeting with the architect and the project manager should resolve the problem. It made absolutely no sense to stop and perform punch-list work now, and even the most unsophisticated project manager would understand, if he would only examine the architect's list.

Roy immediately telephoned the project manager's office and was told he was unavailable until Monday. Roy had a bad weekend but spent his time figuring for the worst. If he had to stop construction and do punch-list work, he would be thrown behind but could still make payroll each week if he delayed payment on the materials bill.

Come Monday morning, Roy was at the project manager's office, bright and early, prepared to go over a reasonable course of action with the manager and the architect. Alas, both had winged their way to cooler climes to discuss the project with the owners. Their exact schedule was not known, but he could check back in a couple of days. So went the week. By the following Monday Roy was to learn that both the project manager and the architect were spending a fortnight in the Rockies skiing and blasting mountain goats. The project was in good hands, and any questions would be fielded by the new executive secretary, who knew absolutely nothing and could not find the bathroom without assistance.

Roy took the bit in his mouth, skipped the punch list, and kept the job on schedule. When the materials people squawked, he exhausted his own funds, borrowed on his home, exhausted his lines of credit, then begged for understanding from his employees and the material suppliers.

When the project manager and the architect returned, there were more long faces, much discussion, meetings, meetings delayed, meetings interrupted, then understanding and verbal promises to pay to date at the next draw, due in a few days.

On the big day, Roy appeared for his check, an expected $1,300,000, and was told by another new assistant that the owners had overruled the project manager and there would be no draw until the punch list and other items were completed. The manager and architect had winged off to argue his case with the owners. Check back next week.

Roy was finished. He could not meet payroll, already a week behind; journeymen and laborers could not work on promises. The material suppliers would not front him another nail.

The numbers are devastating for a small operator. At the completion of ten months' work, Roy was eighty-three percent completed with the project. He had collected only sixty-four percent of the contract price. At the end of the tenth month, Roy had collected $7,700,000. He was owed a ten-month draw total of $9,000,000. He was shorted on the monthly draw $1,300,000. Add the ten percent retainage for ten months, and that is another $1,000,000. His total shortfall of money at the eighty-three-percent completion stage was $2,300,000.

Roy, out of necessity, shut the project down while he tried to negotiate for his money. A new project manager arrived within a few days and told Roy he was off the job if work did not recommence the following morning; the previous manager had allegedly been fired because of Roy. He was handed a letter from the owner's attorney charging breach and demanding performance.

When Roy could not perform, he was handed another letter forbidding him to re-enter the job. His subcontractors were also denied entrance without contacting the new project manager.

Within a few days a new contractor was on the job, and it was humming along. Some of Roy's subs had been retained, and others had been replaced. The new contractor quickly had the project back on schedule; he did not have to fool with the punch list, and the project was completed on time, under budget, and at an enormous profit for the owners.

Roy had, at first, scurried around to lawyers trying to salvage the project. When that failed, he looked for a way to salvage his pocketbook. The first lawyer tried to negotiate with the owner's attorney via telephone, but he was intransigent. He did not want to talk about anything but Roy's alleged breach and the interest the project money was costing each day.

Roy's next lawyer filed a lien on the project and began the long adversarial battle to collect his money. Theoretically the lien would halt selling of the project, but the owner bonded the lien off to clear the title and let his lawyers battle over Roy's $2,300,000.

The owners' lawyers were skilled at using the adversarial system for delay and were able to add months to the litigation by joining all the subcontractors and the materialmen who had filed liens. By this time almost a year had gone by since Roy had left the project. With motion practice, discovery delays, trial-scheduling delays, vacation delays, holidays, nonsense delays, and continuances before them, his lawyer told Roy he estimated it would take the better part of another year to get to trial.

Could Roy recover? Maybe. But the owners were claiming losses because of Roy. There were interest charges, time penalties, increased costs on the job because of Roy's breach, and they charged a ton of inferior work to Roy. Everything that was not perfect on the project was Roy's fault. No matter that it was architectural or engineering; Roy was being countered in the lawsuit for it. By the time the owner's lawyers were finished with their calculations, it appeared Roy owed the owners $700,000.

With another year to go, and a claim for $700,000 from Roy, he asked his attorney to explore settlement. They wanted an offer. Roy said he would settle for his subs being paid and $100,000. They offered to pay the subs--they had already settled cheaply with most of them--and pay Roy $10,000. After a lot of bickering, Roy took $30,000 and walked away.

This is the name of the game: "I owe you two million dollars, and I'm not going to pay you. You use this antiquated legal system and see if you can get your money. It ain't nothing but a lying contest anyway, and I'm a better liar than you. Moreover, I've got the sharpest, crookedest, and, meanest lawyer money can buy. So you get your lawyer, I'll get my lawyer, let's see who wins. I'll bet you $100,000 in attorney fees my lawyer can beat your lawyer and I'll keep your two million bucks. I've got more money than you, I've got your money, and I'm not in a hurry."

You are stuck with the adversarial system to try to force a crook to pay money that belongs to you; you are gambling on who gets your money, not his money. The vast majority of cases settle out of court anyway and generally for less than they are worth; so it is a good bet that the crook will be able to keep some of your money. He will try to make it look like you are the crook, so he is willing to bet he will keep all of your money. He will lie, cheat, delay, or do anything else necessary in the legal system to beat you out of your money. Even if he gets caught, nobody is going to do anything about it. The lies he tells are called his point of view, his position. Every truth you tell will be countered by a dozen clever lies; he will probably win. The adversarial legal system favors the crooks.

"What? You say you are a mob-connected contractor and are not going to waste your time fooling with this ridiculous antiquated legal system? Why didn't you say so? There is no reason we can't work this out without involving a bunch of greedy lawyers. Why don't you come on over and pick up a check?"

CHAPTER V

PERSONAL INJURY

The inequities and overall unfairness of personal-injury compensation in America reflect our failing legal system. Occasionally people with minor injuries receive vast awards. More frequently, people with serious or even crippling injuries receive little or nothing. The failure of the legal system is the primary reason that injured persons are not adequately compensated. If injured persons did not have to contend with a complex, adversarial jury system, injury victims would be better served.

In an adversarial legal system, the injured person's lawyer is trying to obtain as much compensation as possible for the victim, while the wrongdoer's lawyer, frequently an insurance-company lawyer, is trying to pay nothing or as little as possible. At trial, the trier of fact, the judge or jury, is a referee in this little contest. Rather than all parties trying to determine how badly someone is injured and calculating just compensation, they wage a war—and may the best lawyer win! The victim has the wonderful opportunity of being run over again, this time by the system of justice.

The best/worst case example is an automobile accident resulting in a serious soft-tissue injury. A soft-tissue injury is an injury with no bone breaks, invisible on X-rays and sometimes undetectable on other diagnostic machines. It can be a flexation-extension injury commonly termed a whiplash and known in legal jargon as a "whippie."

Typical is the victim rear-ended at a stop light. The victim may state that he or she is not injured, and subsequent medical examination shows no fractures. Days or even years later the victim will begin to experience pain and disability. Some people recover quickly from this type of injury, but others undergo varying degrees of pain and disability for the rest of their lives, so much that careers and life styles are permanently affected.

Automobile injuries almost always bring in an insurance company as the real party in interest either by liability insurance or by uninsured-motorist or underinsured coverage. The insurance industry is shameless in advertising its good citizenship and good faith in the settlement of claims, and there are some companies that settle their claims quickly and in good faith. Some, however, make a policy of litigating every claim, using the legal system to beat their own policy holders, in essence using the system to breach their contracts.

Depending on the local population, which determines the type of person likely to be seated as a juror, one party or the other almost always opts for a jury trial. Judges who hear these cases year after year are not easily deceived about which plaintiffs are injured and which are not. Juries, on the other hand, are more easily deceived as to which persons are faking injuries. I have never seen an injured person uncompensated in a trial before a judge, nor have I ever seen a judge come up with an exorbitant award for a lightly injured plaintiff or any award for one who is outright faking. I have seen a lot of injured persons in serious need of compensation walk away from jury trials without compensation. Some of those denied were represented by tort lawyers that are as good as they come. The adversarial jury system, used to resolve personal-injury cases, favors the insurance company in one jurisdiction and the plaintiff in another jurisdiction. There is no balance in the system: one party or the other is always trying its case with a broken scale.

The economics of the personal-injury legal business is probably the least understood. Most personal-injury work is contingency-contract work. In simple terms, the lawyer manages the case and receives a percentage of the proceeds, usually one third. This aspect of the personal-injury system works pretty well and comes in for justified criticism only when it is abused by individual lawyers who take too high a percentage or simply steal from their clients. In most cases, it is the only way an injured person can afford to pursue a personal-injury claim, especially against a wealthy insurance company in our prohibitively expensive system.

The key players, other than lawyers, in the personal-injury sweepstakes are the doctors and medical professionals. The insurance companies are going to pay claims based on the opinion of the medical experts as to the amount of disability sustained by the victim-plaintiff. If that were all there is to it, it would be acceptable, but that's not the end of it.

The plaintiff has his treating physician, who may or may not be legally sophisticated, testify as to his injuries, his prognosis, and his disability rating. The insurance company hires a doctor who is legally sophisticated and may or may not know much about medicine. The insurance company doctor then conducts what it terms an *independent medical exam*, an IME. The term "independent medical exam" is misleading in that the exam is anything but an independent, impartial examination. It is an insurance company examination of the injured party to determine the nature of plaintiff's injuries or, more likely, to obtain information to allow the examining physician to testify that the plaintiff is not injured.

If the plaintiff's doctor understands the legal game, he can present the plaintiff's claim in its best light. The insurance company doctor, euphemistically called an independent medical examiner, does his best to diminish plaintiff's injuries and may even claim that the plaintiff is faking. The temptation, in a system working like this, is for the lawyers to direct clients to doctors who are sure to testify favorably for their respective clients. To that end, insurance companies have doctors on retainer who examine victims and testify for the insurance companies regularly. Some of these doctors will say anything the insurance companies want them to say. Plaintiff's attorneys, on the other hand, frequently employ a standard plaintiff's doctor. Yet, the frequency with which a plaintiff uses a doctor like this is much less than that of the insurance companies. Generally, the plaintiff's motive in picking a doctor is for treatment, and the plaintiff's attorney has to make do with the doctor who is treating the plaintiff. The insurance company's motive in picking a doctor is for testimony in a courtroom. The chance that the insurance company's doctors are fudging is significantly higher.

Occasionally a plaintiff's lawyer and a doctor are in cahoots to fake test results and to rip off the insurance companies. When these people are caught, there is much publicity, and both lawyer and doctor troop off to prison. When insurance doctors do essentially the same thing, with the tacit complicity of the insurance company lawyers, nothing is done. There appears to be a much higher risk for the cheater who is trying to obtain money than for the cheater who is avoiding payment of money.

Treating physicians frequently find they are spending more time on the legal affairs of their patients than on treating them. After a few sessions of aggressive adversarial lawyers challenging their treatment and expertise to the point of insult, they may become disgusted with the whole mess. Consequently, they raise their fees for testifying to be adequately compensated for having to become involved in a distasteful contest. This results in the people with minor but disabling injuries and little money being unable to afford the doctors; the lawyers will not risk their own money and time on small cases, so these people go uncompensated. Hence the adversarial jury system fails another group of citizens because of expense.

Juries in personal-injury cases are fad oriented, suspicious, and a lot easier to fool than experienced judges. Occasionally plaintiff's lawyers can outrage a jury into awarding millions to a person who is only slightly injured or not injured at all. The insurance companies have countered by spending millions to sell the message that high awards raise rates. I generally ask juries if they believe their verdict will affect insurance rates. The answer is almost always "yes." Jury members frequently vote their own interests in personal-injury cases because the tendency, or fad, is to lessen awards to keep their rates down. It takes only one jury member voting his or her personal interest to drag a verdict far below reasonable compensation.

As the contentiousness and cost of the adversarial jury system increase, responsible lawyers on both sides of the courtroom are seeking alternate problem-solving methods.

One of the methods being used successfully in personal-injury cases is mediation. The parties and their attorneys select a professional mediator, and all appear for a problem-solving session. They present their cases informally. The mediator acts as a neutral party who discusses issues and settlement possibilities with the parties together and separately if necessary. Once the parties reach agreement, the documents are executed and presented to the court for approval and final judgment. Few people walk away ecstatic from mediation, but few stalk away outraged either.

This process is so successful that good mediators, in my experience, have a success rate of eighty to ninety percent. In many jurisdictions, it is the preferred method of personal-injury practice. It is also the first step to privatizing the legal system and illustrates the success of non-adversarial non-jury problem-solving.

Like the remainder of the American legal system, the personal-injury system, approached adversarially, is unsatisfactory. It focuses on a lawyer contest before a jury rather than trying to adequately compensate innocent victims. The adversarial jury system tends to demean the participants; it is not meeting our citizens' needs, and it needs to be replaced.

Legislatures are constantly trying to patch the adversarial jury system by limiting awards, limiting the time period allowed to bring suits, and other less-inspired gimmicks. None of these patch jobs works, and none is likely to work. An adversarial legal system that places a premium on the drama of a trial rather than on fair compensation will continue to fail. We already have an example of a successful non-adversarial method: mediation. Why not change to a legal system that works rather than trying to fix a legal system that does not work?

Wendy

Wendy, a twenty-three-year-old secretary, was stopped at a traffic light on the way home from work. The sun was just setting, and a light rain was beginning to fall. She glanced at her rearview mirror and froze. A large car was roaring toward her, evidencing no attempt to stop, and was almost in her trunk. She picked her foot off the brake but could not get to the gas before impact.

The impact broke her seat and almost drove Wendy into the back seat. The driver of the larger automobile, uninjured, ran to Wendy asking if she was okay and profusely apologizing that he was searching for an address and did not see her. To his credit, he made no attempt to avoid responsibility, readily admitting to the trooper that he was speeding, in excess of forty-five miles per hour, and not watching where he was going.

Wendy was dazed, probably from a light concussion, and her back and neck muscles were stiffening, but otherwise everything seemed to be working. Out of an abundance of caution, the trooper advised that she be transported, and she agreed. At the hospital she was given X-rays and an MRI scan, both showing no fractures or internal body or brain hemorrhage. She was released and advised to consult her physician the following day.

Over the next few months, Wendy's condition improved at first, then deteriorated. Her family physician sent her to a neurologist, who diagnosed her condition as a cervical and lumbar flexation extension injury: a bad whiplash. He was ultimately to give her a six-percent total body disability rating according to American Medical Association guidelines. He wrote that this was all he could give her under the guidelines but that she was even more severely injured. He stated she probably had experienced a total permanent body disability of fifteen percent to twenty percent. A twenty-three-year-old woman had, for recreational and employment purposes, been turned into a seventy-year-old person, and she would be in pain every day for the rest of her life.

As it was to turn out, the other driver disappeared; the insurance company he gave to the trooper had never heard of him. He was uninsured. No matter; Wendy carried an adequate uninsured policy with one of American's bigger companies that advertises its concern and protection of its insured. The company sprung right into action for Wendy, sending an adjuster immediately. He did his level best to get Wendy to settle her disability and pain and suffering losses for $1,500. She refused. She was angry; she was even more than angry; she was furious. She had paid her premiums faithfully, and the adjuster was trying to take advantage of her when she needed her company most. What was all that paternalistic advertising about?

Wendy retained a lawyer & requested that he write a letter to the insurance company. He agreed to try a letter, but he knew it was a waste of time. This company was known among lawyers to take the premiums and refuse to pay claims, even to their loyal policy holders. This company maximized its profits by fighting every claim. Wendy sued.

The suit was not complex; the issues were straightforward. There was no question of liability. This was a rear-end collision, uninsured-motorist claim. The insurance-company lawyers had to find some other argument to the jury to avoid payment than fault for any part of the accident. The question was one solely of damages. Was Wendy permanently injured, and if so, how badly? In fact, to save money, the insurance company lawyers were willing to admit liability.

During the discovery process, the insurance company insisted on peforming an IME, an insurance-company medical exam, euphemistically called an independent medical exam. There was nothing independent about it.

The examination took five minutes, ten tops. The doctor had the history from Wendy's neurologist. He began the exam by asking Wendy a few questions about her condition. He was making notes and reading the history while she was talking. He was not listening to her answers at all. He asked her to repeat the same thing several times. It was not to catch her or see if she was being deceitful; they were simple questions, and he was just not listening. He knew what he was going to testify to before she walked into the office. He felt her neck and asked her to demonstrate range of motion, then felt her lower back. The exam was over.

The judge ordered mediation, normal in these cases. Wendy, with counsel, met the insurance adjuster, with counsel. The company's position was that Wendy was not permanently injured; she was faking. The independent medical examiner concluded there were no objective indications of permanent injury. There was no indication of injury on the X-rays, and the MRI was clean. We already knew that: soft-tissue injuries do not show up on X-rays. He stated that her range of motion was good, that all her pain was subjective; if she believed it was real, she needed psychiatric care.

The insurance adjuster had made it clear to his attorney that he hated all plaintiffs' counsel and would never settle but for a token amount. He told his attorney that his promotions and raises depended on paying little or nothing on claims. It made no difference that Wendy had been a loyal policy holder; he thought her protests were naive and immature.

The company's attorney, visibly pained at the insurance company's position and personally sympathetic, explained what would be his mandate at trial. He told her that he knew she was injured, that her being injured made no difference, that the court was an adversary system and the insurance company refused to pay any claim it could avoid paying; it was his job to try to keep the insurance company from having to pay a legitimate claim, to break its contract with her. What was said in mediation could not be used in the courtroom, so he could be completely candid with her.

As an aside, certain lawyers, to their credit, refuse to work for the more irresponsible of these insurance companies, and they are some of America's biggest companies. This attorney told Wendy's counsel, in private, that he was fed up with this particular insurance company's irresponsibility and was litigating his last case for them.

The lawyer outlined what he intended to do at trial. He would claim Wendy was not permanently injured, that she was either faking, had mental problems, or was symptomatic because she had a pending legal claim for money. He said it made no difference how he personally felt or even if he knew she was injured and he had to lie about it; he had a job to do in the adversarial system.

The insurance company offered Wendy $3700 to compensate her for being six percent disabled. She countered with $30,000, too low for her injuries, but she was fast becoming a realist about the American legal system. The insurance company's final offer was $5000. Wendy refused; it was trial time.

At trial, the venire, the pool of jurors, did not look good. It was summer in the Sunbelt, and many of the wealthy well-educated were back north. Once the striking and selecting was finished, the only person who had been the victim of a whiplash injury was gone. The jury consisted of honest, low-income working people with a low level of education. Most of these people had few assets.

Wendy's doctor, her treating neurologist, was good, but he was rushed. He was between patients and was due at the hospital. He had to keep referring to his notes and made a few mistakes. In contrast, the insurance-company doctor had few patients. His main client was the insurance company. He was paid handsomely for these courtroom appearances and had frequently been an expert witness. He was polished.

Wendy's doctor had been treating her for two years and knew her condition well. He was also an honest man, a big disadvantage in the adversarial trial system. Conversely, the insurance-company doctor was not similarly encumbered by fundamental honesty, a tremendous advantage in our legal system. He was dressed in an expensive suit rather than a hospital tunic. He had little else to do that day. He was articulate and well prepared.

From the information gleaned in a ten-minute examination, he testified the better part of an hour. Yes, Wendy had been in an accident. Yes, Wendy had been injured. He had studied the history. She had fully recovered and could expect no further pain or disability following the lawsuit. He used the hospital X-rays to demonstrate to this unsophisticated jury that there were no objective indicators of injury. This was true, but he used the X-rays to tell a lie, for a deceitful purpose. The summation of his testimony was that Wendy was physically sound. She was either faking pain to make money out of this lawsuit, or she had mental problems. She showed no objective signs of permanent injury.

That the doctor's testimony was untrue was known by everybody in the courtroom except the jury. Of course neither he nor the insurance company would ever admit such a thing. This is the great adversarial jury system we maintain, and deceiving the trier of fact, the jury in this case, is what trials are really all about.

Wendy's lawyers did an excellent job proving damages. Her personal-injury protection had already paid $10,000 in medical and therapy bills. They told the jury her claim was worth at least $100,000 in the marketplace, but nobody in their right minds would suffer these injuries for $100,000. She could no longer bowl; lifting anything on her job was painful; housework hurt; and her love life suffered because of the pain.

Her lawyers told the jury that three times the medicals, $30,000, is generally the absolute minimun that is fair in these cases. Of course the insurance company, really her own insurance company, told the jury she was not really hurt but they would be nice and award her at least $5000. This was the same lawyer who had told her he knew she was injured and apologized for what he would have to say to a jury. He was out-and-out lying to the jury because that is his job and that is what is expected of him in the jury-trial system.

The jury came back with a verdict awarding Wendy damages of $15,000. This was not enough. Under what is called the collateral source rule, what she had already collected as medicals had to be deducted from this. When attorney fees were deducted, not enough for them either for a three-year effort, Wendy was left with less than $5000 to be disabled for the remainder of her life.

What would have been fair? Wendy could be expected to live another fifty years, that is, 18,250 days. One dollar a day for being in pain every day is insufficient compensation, but she was not awarded that much. She would probably spend more than $1000 a year on medicine and therapy for fifty years, which is at least $50,000. The jury was told these things.

The jury thought they did a capital job. One or two wanted to give her the $100,000 but compromised with the one who believed the insurance-company doctor and did not want to award anything. Then there was the juror who worried about the increase in his insurance premiums. The heartbreaker was the one who made only $5000 a year. The award was three years of that person's salary, and that seemed generous. In spite of a good job by Wendy's lawyers, none of the jurors really understood how disabling soft-tissue injuries can be. Whippies are terrible permanent injuries. They are disabling injuries. They are not spurious claims to make lawyers money as the insurance companies would have the public believe.

Three years, a lot of medical expenses, pain, future pain, medical expenses to come, and insufficient compensation. This is the story of the American personal-injury compensation system. As Yogi Berra would say, it's *deja vu*, all over again. If this case were an exception, it could be justified.

It is not the exception; it is the average where this case was tried. In many cases like this one, the jury finds no liability or no damages; they believe the insurance-company doctor. In other cases the jurors are more worried about their premiums than about the injured party. Jury verdicts are based on or influenced by the bull-hockey fed to them by lawyers—lies. In Florida courts in most automobile-accident cases, the jury cannot be told the defendant is insured. The real party in interest, the insurance company, is hidden from the jury and replaced by the driver, who will not pay, who is not the real party in interest but must play the role. It is a gross deception before the jury, and all the judges, lawyers, clerks, and so forth sit around and pretend nobody is lying and nobody is being fooled. We Americans are fooling ourselves. We have a legal system built around the concept of dishonesty, and we pretend it is not so; we are even proud of our dishonest system.

All this overt dishonesty and misrepresentation take place with the absolute and complete knowledge of the trial's participants, and the best liar is the most revered. Worse, we Americans read the first lie over the portals of many of our courthouses when we enter: "We who labor here seek only the truth." Honest citizens should insist that those words be taken down. The American adversarial jury-trial system overcompensates a few injured victims and undercompensates a host of victims. It is a bad system; it is an inequitable system that needs to be replaced.

CHAPTER VI

FAMILY LAW

The courts with jurisdiction over divorce, sometimes called dissolution of marriage or family law, depending on the state, work adequately in some states and less well in others. One universal blessing is that, thanks to our common-law heritage, there is no jury trial available in divorce or family-law matters. It takes little imagination to perceive what a nightmare divorces would be if they were tried before juries.

A common test to show the failure in a system is to exaggerate. The idea of divorce cases before juries is just such a test, and its potential horror illustrates the antiquity of the jury system in America.

The trend in divorce law is toward the no-fault system. No-fault eliminates the necessity of proving grounds for divorce. The parties simply say the marriage is irretrievably broken, then quickly move on to the issues of property division, child custody, and support. This abolishes at least one half of the adversarial issues in divorce cases. Abolishing just one half profoundly improves the operation of the family-law courts. A comparison of the fault with the no-fault system of divorce illustrates how the system of justice improves in any state that eliminates part of its adversarial system of law. Divorce in no-fault states is far less costly to the population and is less emotionally damaging to the parties and their children.

In those states that retain the fault system of divorce, divorces are obtainable but excessively expensive and more emotionally destructive. Those states are gold mines for the divorce lawyers and financial black holes for citizens with domestic problems.

In the fault states the divorcing parties must have legal grounds for divorce. Some of the recognized grounds are adultery, physical or mental cruelty, desertion, lack of support, or a host of other reasons, contrived or otherwise. If none of these grounds actually exists, the lawyers must coach the parties to testify to a legal ground anyway. They actually coach the parties to tell a little white lie, but a lie nonetheless, while under oath. In these cases, the lawyers are actively and openly suborning perjury. The lawyers know they are suborning perjury; the clients know they are being told to lie; and the judges know or should know the witnesses are lying. This winking at lying under oath leads to disrespect for the court system.

The most destructive family lawyers are those who think they must be tough, the most intensely adversarial, to be effective, or who will always address their clients' demands regardless of the merits. Few of these lawyers are wise enough to realize that being smart is generally more successful than being tough. This kind of lawyer should not be practicing family law, but many of them specialize in it.

In the no-fault states more progressive trends are becoming established in family-law practice. The first is toward mediation in divorce matters which, depending on the quality of the lawyers, is either adversarial or problem-solving.

As in personal-injury practice, mediation is a non-binding

settlement conference chaired by a neutral person who attempts to find common ground and persuade the parties to settle the disputed issues between them. If the attorneys are problem solvers, mediation almost always works. Conversely, if one attorney is combative and wants to win an advantage at any cost, the mediation almost always fails.

Another trend is growing among small groups of lawyers who understand the failure of the adversary system and the high financial and emotional costs it exacts from their clients. These lawyers have consciously chosen to avoid or bypass the traditional adversarial process by approaching the opposing attorney in a problem-solving fashion rather than in the traditional adversarial mode. They try to persuade the parties to settle their differences peacefully before a lawsuit is filed. If the opposing lawyer is sophisticated enough to understand the efficiency and value of this approach and is capable of controlling his client, the divorce is generally inexpensive and not so emotionally damaging to the parties and their children.

Few legal problems are as entertaining for the participants as they are for the audience. Accordingly, the more expeditiously a marital problem is resolved, the less money and fewer emotions are expended. Where family law is practiced non-adversarially by good lawyers before good judges, the problems are presented and solved far better than those presented in any adversarial jury procedure in the country. In Florida, it is possible to obtain a divorce in a matter of days at a cost of $500 or less in 1996 dollars. Even the stickiest cases concerning child custody and support can be resolved quickly and inexpensively if the lawyers control their angry clients with good legal advice.

Any experienced divorce lawyer knows pretty much what any given judge is going to do with a given set of circumstances. Two capable lawyers can counsel their respective clients accordingly and reach a settlement. There is no earthly reason, in most cases, to spend months or years and thousands of dollars in these divorce cases. The fighting and deep bitterness generally happen when the lawyers allow them to happen. In most divorces, one or both parties just want out; the lawyers should make it so.

Couple a bad judge with an uncaring adversarial lawyer, and the more promising aspects of family law become an expensive nightmare for the unfortunate citizens involved. While family law practiced by sharp problem-solving lawyers before good judges is a model for our legal system, much family law still suffers from the adversarial practice that is serving our civilization so poorly and serving our families and children even worse.

There is probably no better example than well-practiced non-adversarial family law to illustrate how much more efficient a system can be and how well it works if one can avoid the adversarial jury system.

If we look closely at the non-adversarial non-jury resolution of domestic problems, it can be a partial model and a guide to change the legal systems of America.

Fred and Arlene

A case like Fred's is illustrative of the worst in the adversarial system. His is an uncomplicated case, managed into disaster for him and his family by an aggressive over-adversarial lawyer. In his mid-twenties, Fred was an easy-going man, but estranged from his wife of seven years. They had one five-year-old male child. Fred came to me seeking a simple dissolution of marriage. His wife would maintain custody of the child; Fred would have reasonable visitation; and Fred would pay support. They had worked these terms out between themselves, and I was to put the agreement in legalese to be memorialized by the court: simple.

It is customary to advise, in the document itself, that each party consult an attorney of his or her choice. In this case Fred's wife, Arlene, trooped off to the wrong attorney. Out of the many attorneys she could have selected, she picked the one I would have least recommended, one who made up for her intellectual weaknesses by being as aggressive, uncooperative, and nasty as possible. She is the lawyer people go to when they take the bad advice of searching for a mean attorney rather than an intelligent one.

The agreement I had drawn for Fred and his wife was fair and easy to understand; more importantly, it was what a judge would probably decree should the matter go to trial. In most cases, bright, experienced family attorneys can tell with a reasonable degree of certainty what a judge will do in any given case, after a thorough examination of the facts.

Arlene's attorney looked at the document with suspicion and anger. She advised Arlene that the document was ridiculous and unfair and that Arlene should not let her husband get out of the marriage so easily. Wasn't Arlene being stuck with the child, while hubby would be out chasing younger women? Had she not given seven years of her youth to a man now leaving her? Did she not think that was worth something? For a $1500 retainer, she would make Fred pay much higher child support, and he could also be made to pay alimony. Thus began the battle that was to last over a decade, consuming their youth and their financial resources.

When Arlene responded in anger, Fred decided, or maybe realized, that Arlene would use the child as a weapon. If he wanted to have a relationship with his son, he had better seek custody. We countered Arlene's petition with a petition for custody.

For the trial, we flew in relatives at considerable expense. Both Fred's mother and sister testified that Fred was the better parent and that the child's best interest would be served if Fred had custody. We marshalled friends, neighbors, and co-workers who testified that Fred was the proper person to have primary custody. We had a psychologist as our expert witness. He had examined Fred and had observed the father-son relationship. It was an excellent relationship. He criticized Arlene's use of the child as a weapon. While having temporary custody, Arlene had made visitation difficult and had even denied visitation several times.

The judge ruled that Fred was the proper person to have primary residential custody of the child and that Arlene was entitled to visitation. Arlene's aggressive, nasty lawyer had cost her custody and billed her over $5000. Nevertheless, Arlene stuck with her attorney—they would get even. Over the next several years, we were to be in court semi-annually contending minor issues that should have been resolved between the parties without the assistance of lawyers.

Then a significant turn of events ensued. Fred was offered a job in a distant city that would more than triple his income and give him a job satisfaction he did not currently enjoy. Without thinking of the custody consequences, he packed bag, baggage, and boy; they were off to a new home and new adventures. Predictably Arlene's anger and lamentations shook the courthouse rafters. Arlene was being denied visitation. Not so. Fred had made arrangements for reasonable visitation and was happily paying all transportation costs for his son.

Arlene filed a petition for custody. We had a different judge this time, and he did not see things Fred's way. He ruled that Fred's leaving and working elsewhere was denying Arlene visitation. He changed custody to Arlene and gave Fred visitation. Two trials and many hearings later, these parties were now each approaching five-figure legal fees, and the war was just beginning.

Arlene and her attorney made a great team. Arlene began denying Fred visitation, and her attorney defended this conduct at each hearing. Over the next five or six years, we were in court over Christmas visitation, spring visitation, and summer visitation. The court had to spend its time settling arguments over pickup places, times, costs, and a host of visitation trivia. Over the next decade we trekked through a half dozen judges and thousands of dollars. Arlene was held in contempt five or six times and ordered to pay Fred's attorney fees for denying visitation.

With childhood ending and the teen years approaching, Fred and Arlene's son was an emotional mess. Tugged, pulled, and emotionally battered, he spent his after-school hours in counseling and therapy. The child did poorly in school and had anger that affected his relationship with his classmates.

Finally one of the judges had had enough of Arlene's denying visitation. He returned the child's custody to Fred. Fred, now remarried, with another family, had to shoehorn a child with emotional problems into a crowded household. The child resented his stepmother and was disobedient. Things did not go well. Arlene, living alone and distressed over losing custody, escalated her anger and attacks to a new level. On the verge of losing another marriage, Fred sought counseling.

Fortunately, he picked a wise counselor who quickly grasped the entire scenario. He suggested that Arlene be included in the counseling picture. At wits' end, Arlene agreed. With the help of the counselor, Arlene and Fred finally buried the hatchet. More importantly, she quit listening to her attorney. They both agreed the child would be better off living with Arlene as long as she encouraged a frequent and loving relationship with his father. Fred came into the office; I dusted off the original agreement, and both parties signed it. After over a decade of fighting and attorneys' fees close to $50,000, the parties signed the same agreement they could have signed in the beginning. But things were not and never could be the same as they might have been. Both parties had aged beyond their years; their child would carry emotional scars for the remainder of his life; and the money that could have been invested in a college education for their son educated attorneys' children instead.

I tell Fred and Arlene's story because it represents the worst of the adversarial trial system and the posture that too many adversarial attorneys take. In this case, there is no question in my mind that Arlene's attorney was alone responsible for the disaster that happened to these people. I continually counseled peace, to no avail. It is very difficult not to fight back when each peaceful entreaty is rejected by a legal slap in the face. While the better attorneys are turning away from an adversarial stance in family law, the wife's attorney in this case is still practicing in an aggressive adversarial manner. She sets the tone for a law firm that battles every case to its client's last dollar. When I see that firm name on pleadings, I tell my clients Fred's story or one very much like it.

I have even seen cases in which the parties have turned away from an adversarial stance but the lawyers have insisted on contention anyway. I advise readers to avoid adversarial-type lawyers in their domestic quarrels and to fire them if they insist on continuing conflict when there should be settlement.

I suggest that America turn away from the adversarial trial system in the settlement of family matters and adopt a system similar to the one I have outlined in the appendices.

CHAPTER VII

THE CRIMINAL JUSTICE SYSTEM

Americans believe that our country is soft on crime. This is not true. We have the longest prison sentences in the free world and the highest per-capita prison population in the entire world. In short, we are the planet's most imprisoned people.

Three factors contribute to our misapprehension. Because our prisoners are, for the most part, treated humanely, they do not generally die in prison of diseases or abuse. Criminals regularly beat the criminal-justice system, and the rich can occasionally buy their way out or manipulate the system to impotency with superior attorneys. Finally, press reporting accents these system failures sufficiently so that many youth do not respect a system they may belatedly learn to fear.

For decades the experts have told us that certain arrest with speedy punishment is the most effective way to reduce crime. Law enforcement's use of technology has significantly improved the investigative ability of police, and the future holds promise for more progress and swifter apprehension.

The public blames the courts for our high crime rate and for flooding our streets with violent criminals. The criminal-justice system is not the whole problem, but its failure is partly responsible. So, to some degree, the public is right, but the public is not right in its perceived and articulated reason that the courts coddle criminals.

The courts and the court participants labor mightily and in good faith to solve the crime problem in America; however, they cannot solve the problem, and they will not solve it through the current system.

The criminal-justice system cannot function any better or any faster in an adversarial jury system than can the civil systems we have discussed. In fact, the criminal-justice system is worse; hence, it contributes significantly to our unacceptable crime rate. Unless we change the system and address criminal justice differently, we will continue to fail.

The system, as evolved, requires that a suspect be brought before a judge or magistrate for a first appearance, within a reasonable time following arrest. A bond is generally set at the first appearance, and a date is established for the next appearance.

Following the initial appearance, the defendant is allowed a reasonable time, utilizing the appropriate procedural laws, to discover the charges and witnesses against him. A jury will then be impaneled, a trial held, and the defendant either released or sentenced. The evolved schematic of the criminal legal system looks good and should work smoothly and efficiently. The problem is that it does not work smoothly and efficiently. The criminal legal system is foundering in varying degrees of stress and failure.

There are too few criminal courts, judges, and prosecutors to avail every defendant the full discovery, motion, and trial procedures. Worse, there are probably insufficient resources in many counties and municipalities across the country to make the system work as designed. So how does the system actually work?

Early first appearance with a definite date for a subsequent appearance works fairly well and creates no delay in the administration of the criminal-justice system. The system starts to bog down with motion practice and discovery.

Motion practice is the procedure through which the defense or prosecution asks the court for orders to expand or limit evidence, to more clearly define the charges, to suppress evidence, to dismiss the case on technicalities, or to issue a multitude of other possible orders to adjust the case for trial.

Discovery is the procedure attorneys use to determine the names of the witnesses, examine the evidence, talk to experts, and prepare the case for trial. Here the attorneys, facing combat in the courtroom, gobble up copious amounts of time and resources. After the case works its way through motion and discovery, the decision of trial by jury or plea bargain looms. Now the reason for the stress of the system becomes clearer.

In the best week there are only five working days. Give one day for motions, preliminary, and administrative procedure, only four days remain to hold jury trials. Few judges across the country have only a handful of cases to dispose of each week. Most judges must dispose of dozens of cases each day, and some dispose of 200 or more per week. It is very difficult to do more than one jury trial per day even if there are only one or two witnesses. It is self-evident that if each case went through a full jury trial, the system would back up a year every few weeks.

The system cannot provide a jury trial to each defendant; therefore, the prosecution must plea bargain and the judge must sentence bargain to make the criminal-trial system work. If the criminal has not beaten the system during motion practice, he or she has an advantage knowing the system cannot possibly work as designed. The system cannot try everyone. Therefore everybody starts making deals to the criminal's advantage.

The lawyers engage in a gentlemen's form of legal blackmail. The prosecution postures a vigorous no-compromise position with the prospect of severe punishment. The defense postures a vigorous defense with the threat of a long, drawn-out jury trial. Both threats are real. The potential punishment for any given crime in this country is a long prison sentence. If the defendant wants his day in court badly enough he can have it, but he risks much more than he does if he bargains. On the other hand, the prosecution and the courts do not have sufficient resources to try all the cases, so each jury trial played out to its natural conclusion is costly in time and manpower, severely straining the system. In my twenty-plus years of experience, the trial scenario was not played out in over ninety-five percent of the cases.

By either personal contact between the prosecutor and defense attorney or intervention by the judge, the attorneys begin the process of discussing a compromise. Foremost among the possible tradeoffs, the defense offers to plead to the charge for a lesser sentence or the prosection offers a lesser charge. At maturity, this process amounts to the defense asking the prosecution for its best offer, the defense countering, with the give and take continuing until a deal is struck. This daily process nationwide gives America criminal prosecution by brokerage. The criminal wins, the public loses.

Today's criminal-justice system cannot work any differently. The jury system is so time consuming that there are not enough prosecutors, judges or courthouses to give every accused a full jury trial. The amount of money it would cost to play all criminal defendants through a full jury trial is absolutely prohibitive.

The up side to the brokerage system is that the prosecution at least exacts a quarter of its pound of flesh from each criminal defendant. The down sides are more numerous and are so damaging to our society that they mandate a change.

Violent predatory criminals benefit from the brokerage system by receiving lesser sentences. The public suffers by having these predators loose among us to prey on our property and our loved ones. To solve this problem, the legislatures pass tougher and tougher sentencing laws that are often unresponsive to the real problems and occasionally backfire. With court time and prison space taken up for fad crimes, such as drugs, the dangerous and violent offenders are freed.

When the criminal trial is played out to its logical conclusion, it is too frequently a show-business affair. The prosecutor's job is to obtain a conviction; the defense attorney's job is to beat the case. In the worst-case scenarios, rules are used to prevent the admission of probative evidence, experts are called to cloud issues, and deceptive arguments are tailored to raise reasonable doubts. Somewhere in our journey through the years our legal systems lost the goal of truth and justice and decided to settle for winning and losing.

The adversarial jury system can also produce personal tragedies for the innocent who are caught in its brokerage deals. In the wrong place at the wrong time or falsely accused and facing the possibility of a long prison sentence, an innocent person may find it prudent to plead to something he did not do for a slap on the wrist. This is not a rare occurrence. This happens every day in this country and is recognized in some jurisdictions' plea agreements. A person in many places is allowed to plead "in my own best interest" rather than "guilty as charged."[1] This is a recognition in itself that innocent people are pleading guilty to crimes and that the system does not work as it should.

In those cases in which a compromise or agreement between prosecutor and defense cannot be reached, the defendant goes before the jury as the system has evolved. The difference between today's jury and early American juries is information and prejudgment. Juries today are fickle creatures. Twenty years ago, juries insisted on giving every defendant his day in court. Now juries insist on having their day in court.

Today's juries are products of the information culture and are therefore subject to its fads. Once the public decided that drugs were the number-one problem, the prosecution had only to accuse the defendant of drug involvement and the defendant was almost automatically found guilty. The same has happened with drunk-driving charges or driving-under-the-influence charges. In other words, the juries are trying to get even with the criminals and solve the crime problem at the same time. The result is a jury system that is making a lot of very bad mistakes.

Of course not all the mistakes are against the accused. Many mistakes are against society. Good defense attorneys can occasionally talk juries into believing all sorts of fictions. When that happens, and it happens more frequently than prosecutors like to acknowledge, criminals go free and the public loses.

The failing American criminal-justice system also places undue pressure on prosecutors. The public is frequently outraged and vocal when prosecutors with weak cases make deals with violent criminals in order to obtain at least some jail time. Conversely, insecure prosecutors will file charges on marginal cases to quiet public outcry, thereby placing innocent people in a terrible dilemma.

Every defense attorney is familiar with the prosecutor who strays over the line to obtain a conviction because he believes the defendant is guilty—the philosophy that the end justifies the means. The problem with occasionally straying over the line is that it becomes a habit with most prosecutors who resort to it. All of these stresses and strains are because the system cannot handle the load.

The area of the criminal-justice system that seems to get the most severe criticism is the juvenile-justice system. Like its parent system, the adult criminal-justice system, it is failing in varying degrees. The juvenile-justice system has good things in it and may be the best of an overall bad criminal-justice system. The reason for the failure of the juvenile-justice system and the reason it will not work is that it is built on or, more accurately, piggy-backed on a failing adult system.

Our false perception of coddling criminals in America does its most damaging work here. Our teachers know very little about the criminal justice system; therefore, our schools teach nothing about it. Our marginal youth are not told how horrible their lives will be when controlled by the criminal-justice system and the prisons. Being young, they commit foolish crimes for little reward.

The concept of the juvenile-justice system is to help youth in trouble, but this help leaves them with the impression that the system will do little to punish them, and they are correct. Juveniles who commit felonies are placed on probation and given counseling rather than sent to adult prisons. This concept of help is too frequently carried through numerous felony convictions, some for extremely violent crimes. Since the juvenile system did not treat them severely, young criminals fail to understand that the adult system will do a lot of terrible things to them, and we have another generation of career criminals before they find out. The perception that we coddle criminals and thereby create criminals becomes a self-fulfilling prophecy in the juvenile-justice system. Attempts to help young people are perceived as leniency with the expectation of perpetual leniency, which matures into adult crime. The juvenile-justice system will never work until we reform the adult criminal-justice system.

The legislative reaction to a failing criminal-justice system is to increase prison sentences, and to enact minimum mandatory sentences for selected crimes. These band-aids also fail. Every judge and criminal-trial lawyer can tell horror stories of mandatory sentences being imposed in inappropriate cases and people sent to prison for many years who should not be there at all. A reaction to the drug problem has been the mandatory or long sentence. The result has been prisons overcrowded with addicts, leaving no room for real criminals. The whole dumb faddish reaction backfired and assisted in giving us the highest crime rate in our history.

Reform of the criminal-justice system can help resolve the criminal problem, but it is not the final solution. There are many reasons for crime in America: poverty, guns, unemployment, and family breakdown, to name a few. Reforming the criminal-justice system will not cure these causes, but it will help. The questions we Americans have to ask ourselves is why we maintain a criminal-justice system that does not and cannot work as designed; and why we maintain a system that is so slow and overcrowded that its procedures cannot be fully employed. The usual answer is that it is the system of government designed by our forefathers and that it is the best in the world. It may have been designed by our forefathers, but it does not work very well and is certainly not the best in the world.

In fact, it may be so bad that unless we abolish and replace the adversarial jury-trial system, we will not be able to control crime in America without instituting a police state.

Charley

Our overburdened adversarial trial system frequently allows violent, dangerous, and even mentally disturbed felons back into our neighborhoods after serving only light sentences or even after beating the system altogether. Some of these people should never be free: the serial killers, the violent rapists, and the confirmed career child molesters. Prisons are not nice places, but some human beings either through their own volition or through the demons that drive them cannot live among peaceful citizens. Until or unless we learn to habilitate these people, we must be serious about locking them away from the population forever. The "Charley" of this story is a good example of the failure of our system.

Charley was twenty-eight-years old, about six feet three inches tall and at least 240 pounds—solid. He was considerably less than average in looks and wore thick glasses. His uniqueness was in his eyes and demeanor. Charley made almost everyone uncomfortable. You could sense there was something not right with Charley but could not quite put your finger on it. Charley also had bad teeth and bad breath, and his hygiene was not the best.

Charley's aunt hired me, sight unseen, from afar: after all, Charley had had a lot of trouble in his life. Charley was in jail charged with three counts of aggravated sexual battery—rape with violence or a weapon. Charley had used both.

Just before Christmas, the holiday spirit was in the air and everybody was bustling about doing last-minute shopping. The "girls," all divorced and in their mid-thirties, decided to stop for a last-minute drink before they split for their respective holiday destinations. Off early, 4:00, they drove Betty's Cadillac Seville to a local watering hole.

The place was already crowded, and finding a table and getting drinks was an ordeal, but good cheer was in the air, and anticipation powered the revelry. The girls exchanged flirtations with the neighboring tables and talked thirty-year-old-girl talk. They never noticed the big man at the bar, Charley.

Charley noticed the girls. He watched admiringly, envious of their freedom, comradery, and bubbling gaiety. Charley was alone this holiday season. Charley was alone last holiday season. In fact, Charley was always alone.

Two hours into the festivities, one of the girls checked her watch with a start. Wow! they had over-stayed their intended visit; each was now late for the holiday start, so they busied themselves gathering purses and coats, catching the waitress, and paying the bill before hurrying out into the late-evening chill.

The girls bounded into the automobile, and Betty hit the starter before the door lock. Too late. Charley joined Wanda in the back seat brandishing a large, dark-bladed knife, a marine K-bar. Flashing it first at Wanda, he reached to Carol in the passenger seat, snatched her head back by her hair, and laid the K-bar on her throat.

"Any problems and I kill her. Now back out slowly and drive east."

Betty, having been married to a violent man, had a well-honed sensitivity to acute danger. She was also a very bright lady who thought that cool and calm were the best avenues to survival, given the situation. While Carol began to tremble and cry and Wanda rabbited into the corner, considering the door handle and flight, Betty counseled calm and assured Charley all would comply.

With her foot shaking on the accelerator, Betty backed out and drove carefully along the highway to the deserted countryside between cities.

Once the car was past lighting from commercial signs and street lights, Charley released Carol, warned the girls that he would kill them if they did not cooperate, then turned his attention to Wanda. Wanda started to resist and protest, but one vicious backhand quickly changed her mind. Betty, the level-headed one, was strident in her admonishments to both Wanda and Carol to cooperate.

Charley fondled Wanda and then made her perform oral sex while he caressed her neck and face with the K-bar. After orgasm, he let Wanda whimper in the corner while he turned his attention to the front. He leaned over and fondled each girl's breasts in turn while giving directions to stay on the dark back roads. Twenty minutes into the drive, he directed Betty to pull over. He forced Carol out of the car with him while he stepped a few paces away to urinate. Re-entering the car, he forced Carol into the back seat with him and moved Wanda to the passenger seat.

Charley then made Carol perform sexual acts and continued his stopping and switching for the next three hours. He, in turn, continued to sexually assault all three women.

When Charley first got out of the car, Betty made a pact with Wanda: they would not leave each other; they would all survive or none would survive. At the next stop, Carol and Betty went into the bushes to urinate and discussed running. They decided Charley would kill Wanda and made the same pact to stay together, with one caveat. Once Charley started using the knife, it would be every girl for herself, bail out even if the car is moving.

It was not until Charley was sexually sated that the atmosphere began to lighten a little and the dynamics of the situation could be changed. Betty began a friendly discussion with Charley while she continued to drive. During this conversation, she knew where she was; Charley did not. Betty drove toward a more populated but still unlit area. Once the other girls realized Betty had Charley relaxed and talking, they took hope that they might get out of this situation alive and joined in.

Over the next hour, they learned a lot about Charley psychologically. He was lonesome, with no girl friends, no friends. He just wanted to be like everybody else. The mommy and the hostage in the girls took over as they empathized with Charley and convinced him that everything would be all right. They even convinced him he was really a great lover and that three boyfriendless girls could use a Charley if he was willing to settle for something less than permanent and be faithful to the three of them. He was.

Betty told Charley she had some marijuana in her apartment and they should drive there and party. Charley agreed. Back into the city and bright lights, Carol suggested a drink and persuaded Charley they should all stop at the next nightspot. By this time Charley was convinced he had three girlfriends and agreed.

Charley herded the three girls into a corner table, and Carol immediately excused herself for the bathroom. Betty volunteered to purchase drinks and split for the bar. At the crowded bar she ordered drinks and tried to get the busy bartender to understand they were hostages and to call the cops. She could not get the message across to him in the smoky hubbub. She looked around furtively for a phone, but one glance at the trapped Wanda changed her mind.

Just as the bartender was placing the drinks on the bar, the man standing next to Betty politely interrupted her and inquired, explaining he had overheard her pleas to the bartender. She quickly explained the situation, and he asked her what she wanted him to do. Thinking first of Wanda, she asked him to get Wanda away from Charley. "That's easy," he said.

He walked over to the table, drink in hand, and addressed Wanda in a commanding manner: "Wanda, come here, I need to talk to you." Wanda looked up and bolted past a surprised but unresponsive Charley.

Carol was just returning from the restroom when all three girls found themselves together with a stranger twenty feet from a Charley with his back to them. Without so much as a thank you to the heroic gentleman or a pause to pay the bill, they voted with their feet. They hit the parking lot at a run, piled into the car, hit the door lock, and screeched out of the parking lot.

Once at Betty's apartment they telephoned the police, who not only took half an hour to respond, but reluctantly believed the three girls and even more reluctantly sent a car to look for Charley, who, of course, was gone by that time.

The next day the three gave their statements to an uninterested detective. He did not bother to look at their car, and they could not persuade him to take fingerprints, which he said were useless with no suspect. It was after lunch when the three angry ladies, now more angry at the lack of police interest than at Charley, thought to look in the back of the car for the knife. Sure enough, the K-bar was still on the floor.

Back at the police station, raising hell, they began to get enough attention to have the evidence taken and the car processed for prints. The police only reluctantly did that much and no more.

Betty's brother and Wanda's boyfriend were so angry about the girls' story, they decided to look for Charley. They began that evening at the first bar. Guess what? Sitting at the bar was a man who fit the girls' description of Charley. Sliding up to the bar for drinks and eventually engaging the big man in conversation, bingo! they had Charley. Betty's brother went to the phone and called the girls, who stormed to the police station. The police responded, and that is how I met Charley.

Charley was facing some major-league problems. His bond was prohibitively high, but considering the charges, there was not much we could do about that. The main thing was the possible sentence. Charley was looking at three life sentences. Where he was caught, that meant at least twenty-five years with no chance of parole on each charge.

Considering that the prosecutor had a knife with prints,

Charley's prints in the automobile, and three solid, attractive witnesses, I figured a jury trial would be a disaster. I decided the best strategy was to jump in quickly and cut a deal before the prosecutor and the court invested a lot of time and energy in Charley's problem.

Charley's first break came with the judge. Of all the judges possible, Charley drew the one least likely to have a profound understanding of the Charleys of the world.

I quickly took depositions of the three girls and was as interested in their attitudes as much as in their story, which I already knew. After the depositions, I was able to talk personally in a friendly manner with the girls to see if they would be amenable to some sort of plea. I let them come to the conclusion that nobody had actually been cut and that Charley was just a mixed-up, lonely guy who would probably benefit from psychiatric help. They agreed they would settle for considerably less than life if it was okay with the prosecutor and the judge.

Charley admitted that he had some problems, but minimized them and agreed they would probably respond to psychiatric care. If I could get the prosecutor to accept ten years, he would be out in three or less.

The prosecutor, overworked and underpaid, accepted the idea of ten years and psychiatric care if the girls and the judge would go along. So we pled Charley to ten years.

The judge accepted the plea with the direction to the prison authorities to give Charley psychiatric care. Nonsense. There was no psychiatric care in prison to deal with a man like Charley. The girls did not have a clue about the prison system; the prosecutor cleared another case; and the judge was too uninformed and stupid to see a potential serial killer slipping through the system.

Curious, I had a long talk with Charley in the jail after the sentencing. The culmination of that conversation went like this:

"Charley, would you have cut those girls?" I inquired.

"No, no man, I wouldn't have hurt them."

"Bullshit, Charley." I challenged. Charley hesitated, then looked menacingly into my eyes.

"I would have killed them," he said, then continued, "I've got a real problem. I really need help."

"You know, Charley," I continued, "the psychiatric stuff in prison is bullshit. There's no help in prison. That was for the judge's benefit, to cover the judge's ass. That he was too dumb to know the difference was to our benefit."

"You already told me that," he responded.

"What happens the next time, Charley?" I inquired. He thought for a minute, then looked somberly at me.

"I won't leave any witnesses the next time," he responded. I studied my hands a moment and sighed.

"I was afraid of that, Charley."

Thus ended my contact with Charley but not my thoughts about him. The bargain made in this case is what the adversarial jury system has come to in an America ending the Twentieth Century. This is how it works and how it resupplies our streets with dangerous persons.

I do not know what happened to Charley. Maybe he is okay and the girls he has come into contact with in the decade or so he has now been out of prison are okay, too. But that is not the way I would bet my money. I may have been instrumental in loosing upon the public a wiser serial rapist-killer. I hope not.

If I did, I apologize to my fellow citizens and try to make my amends by suggesting a new legal system that will do a better job of protecting all of us.

NOTES

1. *Plea forms in the state courts of Florida offer the defendant the option of pleading, "I believe that I am guilty," or "I believe it is in my own best interest."*

PART II

THE PLAYERS

CHAPTER VIII

LAWYERS

The vast majority of American lawyers are only incidentally affected by the adversarial jury system because very few actually practice in the courtroom. Many lawyers have only a theoretical understanding of the trial system, and in many cases, are no better informed than the non-lawyer businessperson. Since most lawyers are not directly involved in the adversarial jury system, they do not think to question the system any more than other informed citizens. The only attorneys who have a broad direct knowledge of the adversarial jury system are the lawyers who work directly with the system as either trial attorneys or judges. These trial attorneys are such a diverse group of people with such a broad range of practices and varying degrees of success that they are difficult to categorize. It then follows that America's trial attorneys would each tend to view the efficacy of adversarial justice differently. Some successful lawyers love the combat; others have grown weary with the cost and inefficiency of the system. But as in any other business, initial success as a lawyer may have more to do with money connections and even the law school attended than with native ability.

Few trial lawyers in early America had a formal legal education. They learned the law by reading law with an established lawyer and serving what amounted to an apprenticeship or an internship. The population was small with most lawyers knowing the opposing counsel personally. Being clever was respected, but being slick, dishonest, mean, or otherwise disreputable was frowned upon. Peer pressure was sufficiently strong to control the members of the trial bar. The diversity of subject matter was less, and the body of law was smaller than what lawyers deal with now. The adversarial system worked adequately. That is certainly not the case today. The practice of trial law is now a dog-eat-dog business. The complexities of modern life and the proliferation of lawsuits addressed by swarms of lawyers have overwhelmed our antiquated system. As rural areas in modern America become urbanized, the legal system in those areas begins to fail. The older trial lawyers lament the effect the loss of their provincialism has had on the American system of justice without totally understanding what is wrong. They are offended by the lack of respect they receive from younger trial lawyers and distressed at the public's disdain of the whole legal profession.

Today, trial lawyers receive their training in law schools. Regardless of the law school attended, all law students study the same cases and read the same books. Law schools are differentiated more by tuition costs and by who can get into a particular school than by their curriculum. Law schools use the case method of study, so all law students graduate with a very similar education. Students are taught that our legal system is an adversary system. They are taught that trial law is a tough, aggressive business. There is no criticism of the adversarial jury system as an institution; and if the concept is questioned, I do not know of it.

By the time of graduation, American lawyers take for

granted that the American adversarial jury system is the best legal system in the world. They never question the system, and criticism by foreigners who view the system as slow, ponderous, and expensive falls on deaf ears.

Following the graduation ceremony comes the most significant division of lawyers. One group of lawyers goes into government service and may or may not ever try cases in a courtroom. Many go into an office practice either in large firms or as corporate counsel or do real-estate and probate work, which rarely if ever requires a visit to the courtroom. It is the third group, the trial bar, that works the failing part of the system.

It does not take a neophyte trial lawyer long to realize that trial practice is not a genteel business. The goal in an adversarial system is to win and win by any method that is legal and not unethical. If the problem is solved or the truth inadvertently seeps out in the meantime, that is probably okay too, but that is not the goal.

To that end, a trial lawyer evaluates the case in terms of the legalities or technicalities surrounding the facts. If the client's position is not strong or just plain wrong, the lawyer searches for a technicality to dismiss the opponent's case or to tangle him up long enough to change positions.

A lawyer is mandated by the code of ethics to represent a client to the best of his ability. If the client's case is a poor one, he must still do his best. That translates into trying to the best of his ability, regardless of the merits of the case, to win for his client. To many lawyers, that means taking everything to the ragged edge of ethics and law, and possibly stepping over, but not getting caught. In other words, the trial lawyer's job is to make the jury believe his client's case whether it be right or wrong. In some cases to make the jury believe that which is not true requires deception and foolery. The trial lawyer, in those cases, becomes a trickster, a liar, a flim-flam man, an actor, or a very good lawyer, depending upon your perspective.

A smart, experienced judge, presiding as the trier of the facts, is a difficult animal to fool. A jury sitting as the trier of the facts is, by and large, a lot easier to deceive. A great deal of legal education, continuing legal education, and sage advice from older lawyers is devoted to tricks and technicalities to do just that, to deceive a jury.

Law schools teach and lawyers devise all sorts of little gimmicks for the deception of juries. Courtroom body language and demeanor is just a small example. Lawyers are taught to smile and make light when the testimony against their client is devastating, or to thank the judge when he rules against them on an objection. The main idea is to create an illusion to deceive the trier of fact. The best trial lawyers are actors, creators of false images. There is no reason to do these things except to deceive a jury. So, in a jury trial, the lawyer with the just case must laboriously get his case across to a jury while the opposition tries to stop the testimony by objections or other devices to deceive the jury.

Law students are taught to culture their clients; make the bad guys look good, the good guys look bad; give reality to illusion; and make the illusion fit their cases. I always tell my clients that a jury trial is like a football game. It looks like a game of yards, but often it is a game of inches, "game" being the appropriate word. The good trial lawyer tries to gain every inch and keeps a running scoreboard in his head as to whether he is ahead or behind on points.

A lawyer with a weak case, or one in which delay is a financial or strategic advantage, is prudent to ask for a jury trial. He can delay a case through a wise motion practice, sometimes for years. In front of a jury he may use a clever bag of tricks to deceive the jurors into believing his side of the argument, thereby functioning within the system but perverting the ends of justice. Superior advocacy is frequently equated with the biggest or most successful misrepresentation to the jury. Of course, many patrician lawyers will resent words like this and maintain that representing their client's point of view is legitimate, not misrepresentation to the jury, nor is it creating an illusion. Representing their client's point of view is certainly legitimate, but to deny what all trial lawyers are doing in these courtrooms is simply dishonest and self-deceptive. It is a pity that we have a legal system in which creating an illusion or a falsehood for the jury is venerated.

The worst lawyers to try cases against in the courtroom are those who equate nastiness and pure contentiousness with good advocacy. They are also the ones who will tell the biggest lies to the jury and misrepresent cases to the judge. They are generally the least effective lawyers, and dealing with them is unpleasant. There is a lot of this type of conduct in our crowded courtrooms today. It leads older lawyers to take early retirement if they can afford it.

If familiarity and peer pressure restrained the conduct of early American lawyers, the relative anonymity of modern lawyers places less restraint on conduct. In this crowded communication age, a lawyer can be rude, unfair, or even dishonest with impunity to an out-of-town lawyer or even a cross-town lawyer he will have to deal with only once in his career.

I contend the adversary system works in favor of the dishonest litigant and the unscrupulous lawyer. It is easier to be destructive than constructive. It is easier to tear down than to build, therefore easier to obstruct, delay, and destroy than to construct, particularly to construct a positive legal case. It is easier to be a combatant and let the judge or jury decide than to be a problem solver.

Most American lawyers are hard-working, honest people who are trying to represent people winding their way through the labyrinth of the American legal system. That the adversarial jury system makes it easier for the few unscrupulous lawyers to prevail when they should not is terribly frustrating to ethical lawyers.

Most good lawyers are not fearful of presenting their case before a jury. An understanding of the law and careful preparation make jury trials an easy job. What all trial lawyers are fearful of is a trial by ambush. A fact his client has failed to tell him or a law or case he has overlooked can lead to catastrophic defeat. With thousands of laws and millions of cases, nobody can know it all. In our adversary system there is no lawyer who has not been ambushed or surprised in the courtroom. There is no lawyer who has not lost a case because of a surprise. If a lawyer claims it has not happened to him, he has not tried many cases. Every experienced trial lawyer can tell tale after tale of surprises, mistakes, bad rulings by the court, and unfair or stupid jury verdicts. Our system is so rule and precedent bound that, in the heat of trial, there are few provisions for correcting catastrophic mistakes or omissions, truth and justice be damned. It is this fear of the unknown and the inability to rectify errors that make trial practice a high-stress business and lead to early retirement if not early death.

This fear of ambush causes lawyers to overprepare and legal bills to skyrocket. It is bad enough for the suffering public to pay exorbitant legal fees when they feel they are being given a fair trial. When clients have to pay expensive legal bills and feel the system is not working, they become outraged, and that is the state of the adversarial legal system in America today. We are seeing this rage expressed sometimes by gunplay in our courtrooms, hence the necessity for expensive security in our courthouses. This also means everybody loses in our system except the dishonest litigants and that handful of lawyers who are interested only in large fees, their clients and the public be damned.

Most trial lawyers are cynical about juries and the system in general. By and large trial lawyers intuitively do not like the system but do not know why and have never thought to question this most fundamental of our institutions in terms of substantial change.

Ours is an inefficient and failing legal system. Any system based on the art of deceiving the trier of fact, the judge or jury, and giving the advantage to an unscrupulous lawyer and his lying client is fatally flawed. A more complex society with more and more people will see increased adversarial, malicious litigation. In turn, lawyers will be held in more contempt by a broke, frustrated clientele. Lawyers love to chide the medical profession by pointing out that we lawyers were writing the Declaration of Independence and the Constitution when the doctors were bleeding people. The doctors would do well to respond that today, they are close to understanding the very nature of life, and lawyers are now bleeding the people. Sadly, we lawyers have not changed the system very much in the two hundred years of our national period while the rest of society has marched on past.

Our early American adversarial jury system is incompatible with contemporary America. The lawyers who work in the system have not changed it because they have not thought to question it. As a result, contemporary trial lawyers are taking the full blame for the failure of an inadequate legal system, and things are going to get worse.

Richard D. Sparkman

CHAPTER IX

JUDGES

If there is any way to make the adversarial jury system of America worse, it is to garnish it with a single omnipotent judge—at least omnipotent in the judge's particular courtroom.

All judicial selections in all countries have always been, and will continue to be, political. Judges are either appointed by elected officials or elected. A person may be the best judicial material on the planet, but that person will never sit a judicial bench without some political connections or political capabilities. This does not mean that the political process cannot produce great judges, because it does. It does mean that judicial seats are not necessarily attained by merit.

Nevertheless, most judges in America are hard working and honest. Many are overworked. While I have never met an omniscient judge, most become knowledgeable and proficient in at least one and sometimes several fields if they work hard and stay at it long enough.

Occasionally, a born judge comes along. But they are few, and like any other segment of our population, judges range from excellent to terrible. The vast majority are average, and it is the average judge that presides over most American courtrooms. These judges are good, but they are not good enough, by themselves, to run any legal system. They certainly are not good enough to save, or even adequately operate, a failing adversarial jury system.

These average judges are not bad people. American law is too complex; our life situations, psychology, and general problems are too complex and diverse for any one judge to understand and adequately address. This concept is recognized by default in our appeals systems. No appeals court in this country is run by the single-judge system. Appeals courts are paneled by three to nine judges, depending on the court.

This observation begs the rejoinder that only the serious or major legal questions ascend to the appellate court. We might amend this observation to say that only the serious or major legal problems of the financially able ascend to the appellate court. The middle-income citizen probably considers his or her problem serious, or he would not be in court in the first place. These people cannot afford expensive appeals, but as citizens, they deserve the full consideration of our legal system. They do not get that full consideration because of economics.

When citizens are before one of the few really good judges, they receive an adequate hearing and a good decision. When they stand before the vast majority of judges, they receive something less than excellence. When citizens must present their cases to one of the few fruitcakes on the bench, his decisions can destroy people's lives.

There are enough bad-to-horrible judges in our courts to drag the adversarial jury system to the depths of ridiculousness. Stack an uninformed, unwilling jury on a couple of dishonest, aggressive lawyers and grace it with a stupid, opinionated judge, and the recipe for the trial of your life's most serious problem is complete. This does not happen all the time, but it happens somewhere in America every day. This system failure is the reason many judges are terrified of the public and lock themselves in fortress courthouses.

We, the people, are entitled to better. It is difficult to assemble three dumb judges in any one place. If we move to a three-judge system for all proceedings, we will have a collective wisdom that will go a long way toward sandwiching the bad judges and, by conference, reaching correct or at least better decisions. While three average brains will not replace a brilliant one, the collective education and training of three judges will significantly raise the percentage of correct calls by the courts in our country.

It is philosophically intolerable that we, as the great collective democracy, subject ourselves to a single-judge system. Our judges rule as potentates in their respective spheres of influence; and we, a people who believe in the limitation of power and checks and balances, tolerate this anomaly to all our concepts.

We must replace our single-judge trial court system with a three-judge system. Then no judge can present himself or herself as omnipotent.

Jack's House

Trying technical cases before juries is risky, but the risk doubles when the judge does not understand the issues or even the court's own procedures adequately.

Jack contracted to have his house built beside a manmade canal. He was not familiar with the area, having recently arrived from a neighboring state. In Jack's prior location, the topsoil was solidly supported by underlying bedrock. Not so for the house he was contracting to build. The land had been manufactured from a saltwater-marsh swamp by dredging canals and pumping the fill to make upland. In other words, the high land was sitting on muck, water, and sand.

During negotiations for the home construction, the question of a foundation was discussed with Jack by the contractor. His choices were piles, a slab, or footers underlying a stem wall. The contractor recommended piles, saying an engineer had recommended piles for construction in the area. With no further explanation about the piles or the engineer's recommendation, the conversation moved on to costs. The piles would significantly add cost to the construction of the house, increasing the price maybe a third or more.

Jack was familiar with footers and stem walls and could not afford the piles. He was given no details about the engineer's recommendation of piles nor any specific advice by the contractor. Jack chose the footers and stem walls. The contractor had Jack sign a foundation selection containing a hold-harmless clause that would absolve the contractor from any responsibility for the choice. That the contractor knew the conditions of the area, that Jack did not, and that his choice was potentially disastrous, there was little doubt.

The hold-harmless clause, an unusual clause in a contract of the type in the area, itself was evidence that the contractor knew the danger and was covering his backside. Additionally, the contractor had written into the selection-hold-harmless document that Jack had been advised of the engineer's recommendation. He had been told, but not in any meaningful way. Nevertheless, the document existed, and it was graced with Jack's signature. The house was built on stem walls placed on footers.

Jack and his lovely family moved into a beautiful dwelling by a waterway, and began enjoying their new home in the sun. The contractor was still completing punch-list items and had not received the last draw when the first cracks appeared in the garage. The contractor diminished the importance of the cracks and hurried over to fix them, demanding the balance of the contract money being held by the bank. Jack was prepared to authorize payment and promised to do so on Monday; then on Sunday morning cracks appeared in the ceiling over the staircase.

Jack telephoned the contractor, who promised to fix them, but wanted his money first. Jack refused, and the contractor became angry and nasty, and threatened to sue. Jack did not need litigation; Jack did not need problems; Jack wanted to live in peace, but problems were now stalking Jack. Jack, the next morning, while collecting his paper and exchanging pleasantries with his elderly neighbor, mentioned the subject foremost on his mind.

The neighbor, an unassuming retired man, listened carefully, then, to Jack's surprise, explained in detail Jack's problem, supplementing his explanation with technical data. The neighbor had been a quality builder, had carefully watched the construction of Jack's home and daily discussed with his wife of some fifty years the problems he anticipated the new owner would have with the house. By the time Jack walked back in to have his coffee, he knew the mistake that had been made, the future of the house, and the necessity of consulting an engineer.

It did not take Jack's engineer long to understand the problem either; he had seen a lot of irresponsible building on the fill along these canals. He explained to Jack that his house was doing two things at once. It was differentially settling and it was migrating. Differentially settling Jack understood, but migrating? Migrating where? Well, the house had multiple personalities. The north wall was beginning to move north; the south wall was aiming for the tropics; the west wall was headed to California; and the east wall was interested in Africa. The house was going to collapse: it was just a matter of time, but not a great deal of time. To use military jargon, it was moving out smartly.

Confronted, the contractor produced the foundation-selection document containing Jack's signature and demanded his money. Jack again refused to authorize the bank to pay the last draw of $20,000. The contractor's attorney wrote a threatening letter to Jack and his wife demanding payment within ten days or he would sue.

Jack brought the letter to me along with the engineer's preliminary report and sought my advice. After studying the matter for ten minutes and discussing Jack's circumstances and options for another ten minutes, I advised, "Don't pay." It did not take a lot of study; I had been down this road before. Irresponsible construction in the Sunbelt was not news, and most of the people victimized cannot afford the financial loss nor the inevitable lawsuit. I told Jack to go to the bank and explain his dilemma, obtain the funds to repair or at least stabilize the house, based on what his engineer advised, and let the contractor sue. That is the path he chose.

The contractor sued and demanded a trial by jury. I groaned: another technical case before a lay jury. Then I saw the judge assigned; I groaned again. I feared bad rulings and strange decisions. The judge was not to disappoint me.

After all the normal suit preparation, taking depositions, producing documents, inspecting the site, and hiring experts, we came to the trial. It was winter in the Sunbelt, and the snowbirds had flown south. The jury was not too bad. In fact, we had some well educated and even technically educated people sworn as jurors. I felt much better. The trial proceeded smoothly with the contractor's attorney arguing that the foundation choice was made by the owner and that he had signed a hold-harmless clause. I argued the superior knowledge of the contractor and the state law, which clearly placed the responsibility on the contractor. Neither side contended the house was not in distress.

It was a question of placing fault and awarding damages or the balance of the contract price to the contractor.

By the time the testimony was completed, the jury clearly understood the facts of the case. Both sides had been able to present all the testimony and evidence necessary to establish their respective positions. This left the posture of the case as it should be. The facts were before the jury awaiting the judge's instructions on the law to enable the jurors to apply the applicable law to those facts and render a verdict. Now entered the reason we need to abandon the single-judge system in our trials.

It is the responsibility of the lawyers to prepare the instructions for the judge to read to the jury. At what is called a charge conference, the attorneys proffer their instructions to the judge, and after argument over their legality, the judge makes his decision to accept certain instructions and reject others. These accepted instructions are then read to the jury at the end of the trial as his charge to the jury on the applicable law of the case.

It is customary for the attorneys to urge the judge to read instructions that lend a favorable legal slant to their respective positions, and that is what took place here—except there was an anomaly in this case. Opposing counsel and I understood each other's proffers although we had several significant disagreements. The problem arose when the judge did not appear to understand either of us. He suggested we were both confused and suggested something entirely different.

A judge taking a position like this is not altogether unusual, except that in this case, neither counsel understood what he was talking about. He told us what he wanted and directed us to go, together, and write the instructions. I hoped the other counsel understood the judge, because I did not. Unfortunately the other counsel did not understand the judge either. We could not write the instructions nor the verdict form, and we reported our failure to the judge.

He was much annoyed with us and explained again. Again I did not understand him, and looking at opposing counsel, knew he did not understand either. I made a suggestion. I would bring my secretary, and the judge could dictate his instructions and the verdict form to her. The judge agreed. My secretary of some twenty years drove to the courthouse, took the instructions in shorthand, and transcribed them.

When she returned to the courthouse with the transcript, the judge was pleased. The instructions and the verdict form were exactly what he wanted. Try as I might, I still did not understand his instructions, and the verdict form made no sense to me. Opposing counsel was equally confused.

To an alert, attentive, unconfused jury, the judge read these muddled instructions and presented a confusing verdict form. By the time he finished, the jury had clearly lost its confidence—they looked distressed.

To be expected, the jury brought back a verdict that was a model of confusion. It appeared to say that Jack did not have to pay the $20,000 but the contractor was not responsible for the foundation flaw because of the hold-harmless clause. Jack and I did not like the way it read but were willing to accept the verdict. Opposing counsel was not as pleased.

By happenstance, the opposing counsel heard that the jurors had been confused during their deliberations, had understood neither the instructions nor the verdict form and just marked it as best they could. He did something forbidden, but understandable under the circumstances. He telephoned the foreman of the jury who admitted that they had not understood much of what the judge said and that the verdict form made no sense.

Opposing counsel made a motion to question the jurors, and the court subpoenaed the jurors to the courthouse for examination. The first juror was placed on the witness stand in the presence of the judge, the attorneys, and the parties. The rest of the jurors were sequestered, and were not allowed to hear each other's testimony. Not surprisingly, the jurors admitted that they had been confused and that their verdict had been a guess. They placed the blame for their confusion clearly on the instructions and the verdict form. The court set aside the verdict and ordered a new trial.

The greatest insult came following the judge's order for a new trial. He admonished and lectured both attorneys. He said had we been better prepared, this would not have happened. Had we spent as much time preparing for trial as for this hearing, the verdict would have stood. Both of us took the unwarranted criticism silently, but neither of us will ever forget it.

It was the most unfair criticism I have ever received from a court. For trial, both counsel were well prepared, and we both tried a good case with few, if any, mistakes. The mistakes rested solely with the judge, and the jurors had just finished saying so. Now this judge had the temerity to blame the mistrial on counsel. I generally speak my mind to judges; we attorneys have the right and the duty to do so; but I was stunned into silence by the effrontery of this judge and so was opposing counsel.

Now we had to do the trial all over again. After a year of preparation, thousands of dollars, and great emotional distress, we had to retry the case because of the judge. I still do not know how to characterize what he did, nor why he did it. Both parties told counsel they would not participate in a second trial. They were both financially and emotionally exhausted. They let the verdict stand and went their separate ways.

Admittedly, the judge's decision or misconduct in this case was extraordinarily loathsome from an attorney's point of view, but a judge like this will spend a career wrecking lives. It would be almost impossible to find three judges who could collegiately make such an egregious ruling as in this case without having smoked hallucinogens. If we sandwiched our bad or ignorant judges between good ones, our courts would function more smoothly and be more efficient.

Personality Disorder

Even good judges make mistakes—occasionally serious mistakes. It is not good enough to have the right of appeal. In our overpriced legal system few can afford the trial, never mind an appeal that adds expense by multiples; so courts have to get it right the first time. When they err on the first shot, citizens' lives are adversely affected, and these mistakes significantly diminish the quality of life for a lot of people. That is why we should not trust these decisions to a single-judge system.

Stephanie had been married for ten years and was the mother of three elementary-school-aged children. To her family, her friends, and her fellow employees, Stephanie had a good marriage with a loving husband. If they had problems, they were unknown outside of her household. But Stephanie's life was not as it appeared to outsiders.

Stephanie's husband was narcissistic; the family did what Bob wanted to do, never what Stephanie or the children wanted to do. If a family decision was to Bob's liking or Bob perceived it to be in his best interest, that was the family decision. Bob dressed well, had a better than average wardrobe; Stephanie had the clothes she needed for work, little more. Stephanie did not need makeup; she already had a husband; the only purpose for makeup was to attract men. Earrings were for the same reason, so she was not allowed to purchase them. Essentially Stephanie's wardrobe consisted of jeans, t-shirts, shorts, sandals, and sneakers. In ten years of marriage she had never bought a dress.

Bob had never taken the wife or children to a restaurant for dinner; Bob said he did not like to eat out. Bob ate out, of course, but that was for socializing with his friends or for business purposes—wives and children not welcome. The family had never been on a vacation. Bob went to events with his buddies, but those were all male trips, not suitable for wives and children. Stephanie's life consisted of going to work and coming home to take care of her husband and children. She was Bob's servant at home, and he never assisted in domestic chores.

To people who did not know Bob well, he appeared a regular guy. Stephanie knew a different Bob. She knew a man who was basically dishonest, would lie about anything if it was to his advantage, and would steal from his employer, family, or friends as long as he had little chance of ever being detected. He was smart in his criminality; he was never detected. Bob was a very bright man, and he never took a chance with his dishonesty. Only his wife knew how dishonest he was: it was a marital secret.

Bob never went out and drank or frequented bars, but he drank. As the years rolled by, Bob drank more and more and became abusive. At first he just pushed Stepahnie around and punched holes in doors and walls. But, as his drinking progressed, he became increasingly abusive, and occasionally punched Stephanie as well as the doors.

Stephanie hid the abuse; she would have been embarrassed to let anyone know how she lived. She had married Bob in her teens partly to escape from an abusive home. While he was not her ideal man, what he offered seemed better than her parents' home, and it had been, for a few years. She certainly was not going to run home to "I told you so."

Over the years Stephanie came to realize that other wives did not live under these conditions and actually indulged themselves by going to the hairdresser, a trip Stephanie had never made. Eventually a friendship grew between Stephanie and a man at work. He treated her with respect and listened sympathetically when she finally unloaded her unhappiness.

Things came to a head when Stephanie found out that husband's evenings out with the boys were not always with the boys. Bob had had a girlfriend for years. He had never been reluctant to purchase dresses, cosmetics, and jewelry for her. After Stephanie discovered the girlfriend, she began having an affair with her male friend.

When Bob found out, he went ballistic. His affair of years was acceptable but not hers. He beat her up, took his belongings, and moved in with his girlfriend. He then began a systematic campaign of terror against Stephanie. Her car was vandalized; the house was broken into and ransacked; and she was harassed by hangup telephone calls. After most of the windows in the house were broken, it became uninhabitable, and she asked Bob to take the children until she could find a place to live. Bob took the children, replaced the window glass, and moved back into the marital home. Stephanie moved in with her male friend.

Once Stephanie set up house, she asked Bob for the children, and he agreed to bring them to the County Fair so she could take them to live with her. Bob had never used the children as anything but slaves, and they were glad to be going back with their mom.

At the fair, Bob, true to his word, had brought the children, but he had no intention of letting them live with Stephanie. Bob was an auxiliary policeman, and he had several of his buddies near where he told Stephanie he would meet her with the children. At the exchange point, Bob had his girlfriend along, herding the children. This angered Stephanie, and she started to come unglued when Bob provoked an argument. When Stephanie reached for her youngest child's hand, Bob's girlfriend snatched him away from her; and when Stephanie grabbed the child back, the girlfriend shoved her. The other woman's grabbing her child then pushing her was too much: the mommy instinct to protect her young went wild, and Stephanie clobbered the girlfriend.

The auxiliary cops jumped all over Stephanie, threw her onto the ground with the elephant feces, arrested her, and carted her off to jail. Bob seemed pleased by the events; no doubt he had engineered them, and the program came off better than he had expected. By the time Stephanie came to my office, she was on probation for battery, and Bob had filed a petition for dissolution of marriage. He demanded custody and claimed that Stephanie was an unfit mother because of a violent criminal record and that she was an adulteress, living with a strange man.

She was not very far into her story before I could have completed it for her. Any lawyer who has practiced family law for two decades has seen a lot of Stephanies, and their stories are similar. There is, of course, the corresponding male story when the wife is the counterpart of Bob, but this is Stephanie's story.

Observing Bob in the early proceedings and listening to how Stephanie had lived all these years, I had my thoughts about Bob. Trial lawyers see enough of the same conduct over and over that they become empirical psycholgists. I thought Bob might have a diagnosable psychological problem; more specifically, I thought he might have an anti-social personality disorder. These people used to be known as psychopaths, but the title of this pathology has changed, if their conduct has not.

I asked the judge for a psychological or psychiatric evaluation of Bob, and his attorney, not having a clue what I was looking for, readily agreed as long as Stephanie would submit to the same evaluation. I was not worried about Stephanie. In twenty years, I have asked for this evaluation only when I was reasonably sure of the problem. I am proud to say I have yet to miss on this amateur diagnosis.

Sure enough, Bob was disagnosed with anti-social personality disorder. To emphasize the point, this was a diagnosis, not a suggestion nor an indication: this guy was a full-blown psychopath. So we went to trial after a year of motions, delays, and unacceptable fees and costs that neither party could afford. The only curve we had in the proceedings was an ill-advised program dreamed up by one of the judges. He had established a child-advocate program that consisted of a bunch of untrained amateur busybodies who would run around interviewing some of the parties and then testify at trial who was the proper parent to have custody of the children.

Many psychopaths are such accomplished actors and intelligent liars that they fool even the professionals. To fool these amateur court advisors was no big trick. The psychopaths who interviewed with them batted close to a hundred percent to my knowledge, and I had considerable knowledge about their batting averages.

Bob put on his witnesses who, expectedly, all said he was a wonderful guy, the most caring of husbands, and a model father. His girlfriend, now living with him, testified that their relationship was strictly platonic until Stephanie, horrible bitch, became an adulteress. I did not press the issue; I did not think the judge was that dumb.

Stephanie's witnesses testified she was a wonderful wife and a model mother, and had never strayed until Bob was caught straying. The judge was impressed with neither of these scenarios, having heard the same testimony so many times he could rule on it in his sleep. Then came the child advocate as a court-called witness. The child advocate had filed his report only minutes before the trial started, so neither party had had an opportunity to inquire or prepare; it was always a surprise one way or another. This program was later abolished because of its non-professionalism and abuses.

In any case, the child advocate found Bob to be the proper parent to have primary residential custody of the three minor children. I cross-examined. Had he read the psychological report? No. Did he know what anti-social personality disorder meant? Thought he had an idea, but could not explain. Did he know Bob had a diagnosis? No. Did he know what that might mean for the children's future? He did not have a clue; Bob seemed to be such a nice guy; Stephanie was living with another man, and she appeared to be overemotional during the ten-minute interview he had conducted. And Stephanie had a violent criminal record. Bob had seemed intelligent and stable during his ten-minute interview, and he had no criminal record. He was certainly the proper party to be the primary residential custodian of the children. He recommended that the court award Bob custody.

I had prepared for this eventuality. I had subpoenaed the examining psychologist. The psychologist, who was employed by and did testing under the supervision of a psychiatrist, explained his diagosis and his testing methods, and discussed personality disorder. He also told the judge that the children should not be placed with a personality-disordered person. His recommendation was that Stephanie be selected as the primary residential custodian of the children. I then called another psychologist, a man who specialized in family practice and who had a profound understanding of personality disorder and its effects on children.

I took the psychologist carefully through the pathology and had him relate it to the raising of children. Under no circumstances should these children be placed with the father, the man testified. The judge appeared to be listening and appeared to understand. When the testimony was finished, the judge ruled that the children should stay with the father. He had made his decision based on a ten-minute interview by an untrained amateur and in the face of copious professional opinion to the contrary. He obviously did not understand personality disorder, and Stephanie was a woman living with another man, and she had a criminal record (the incident at the fair.)

A catastrophic mistake? Yes. Why? I do not know other than that I had never observed this judge dealing with personality disorder and am sure it meant nothing to him. I had planned for that problem, hence the two psychologists who baby-stepped him through the pathology. I knew other judges in the same courthouse had a reasonable, if not a profound, understanding of this disorder. I had been through this drill before and had never had a judge fail to understand the problem. A large percentage of the persons who stand before our judges are personality disordered, but very few judges understand what they are dealing with unless lawyers bring experts to testify and explain. Unfortunately few lawyers do this, so we have judges who preside for decades without ever understanding the personality disorders standing before them. I have made a practice of using experts in these cases, when my clients can afford it.

Had I had any two other judges from the same circuit, it is unlikely that the children would have been placed in the custody of a personality-disordered person. In most cases it would be almost impossible to pick three judges who could so badly miss the point. Cases like this are the reason I advocate abandoning the single-judge system.

The issues before our courts today are too varied and complex for a single-judge system. Few of our judges have a broad enough background to preside over such diversity with excellence. Maybe a few very intelligent judges have gained the experience by the time they retire, but the political process places few of these on the bench. Frequently the people who end up on the bench were mediocre lawyers at best or had little or no trial experience. Others have had a very narrow experience or worse, a narrow education, so many of the machinations of society are lost on them. A typical example is the prosecutor who is appointed to a judicial position after prosecuting criminals for ten or twenty years. Inevitably that judge goes to the civil courtroom to hear cases controlled by law he or she knows absolutely nothing about or has not even thought about since law school. It is not amusing to see the mistakes these judges make. They wreck lives as surely as a family physican thrown into a series of complex surgeries having not even thought about such things since medical school.

If this practice were occasional or unusual, it would still be unacceptable when it is your future on the line. But this is the rule, not the exception. Few of our judges are qualified to sit on the bench alone at first, and some never become qualified. We need to change this system.

Richard D. Sparkman

CHAPTER X

BAR ASSOCIATIONS

The Petition of Florida Bar Ass'n et al., 40 So. 2nd 902, Supreme Court of Florida, en Banc. The date, 7 June 1949, references the formation of a bar association in twenty-seven previous states as part of its rationale in forming the Florida Bar Association. The Florida Supreme Court's opinion goes on to justify granting the petition to integrate: *integrate* in this case means to form one bar association from all the county and city bar associations, by citing noble purposes and intentions:

> So the purpose of bar integration is in no sense punitive and there is not a case on record in which it has been employed as a legal strait jacket for disciplinary purposes. In some states it has no part whatever in disciplinary measures. In the states where bar integration has been adopted its major energies are directed to projects designed to improve the administration of justice, projects that awaken an interest in the science of jurisprudence, that stimulate professional interest and that give the bar a just concept of its relation to the public. In some states the question of unlawful practice of the law, educational qualification for admission to the bar,

and the discipline of members for unprofessional conduct, have been included in the integration agenda, but they are incidental to the major energies of the integrated bar.[1]

If the nationwide integrated bar movement, which began in the 1930s, had as its primary purpose the improvement of the administration of justice rather than discipline and licensing, the movement is failing in its primary purpose.

America's bar associations have not been on the cutting edge of social change. That is not to say that lawyers, as individuals, have not led in the struggle to fulfill America's promise of equal protection of the laws, because they have. It is to say, unfortunately, that bar associations have become the conservative protectors of the adversarial jury system of justice. Modern bar associations exist primarily to regulate, discipline, educate, and image their lawyer constituents rather than to advance the science of jurisprudence. The state bar associations are responsible for qualifications establishing the admission and licensing of new lawyers to practice before their state courts and the continuing regulation and discipline of their lawyer constituents. Far more resources are expended in the bar's role as a gigantic complaint department for disgruntled litigants than are expended on the science of jurisprudence.

Nevertheless, the continuing legal education function performed by many state bar associations is impressive. The Florida Bar has mandatory continuing legal education that works well and is a valuable undertaking for both the lawyers and the public.

Within the state bar associations are thousands of lawyers struggling nobly and mightily to find ways to make America's adversarial jury system work, even with one judge per court. These hard-working, dedicated lawyers fail daily, they fail weekly, and they fail yearly. They cannot succeed in making the adversarial jury system work without utilizing non-adversarial, non-jury methods, and that is the trend. Bar journals and magazines are replete with articles extolling alternative dispute-resolution methods such as mediation, arbitration, and various forms of abbreviated trials.

Leave it to simple reasoning: If America's dispute-resolution systems, the courts, were working, why should America need alternative systems?

Bar-association leaders in their monthly speeches and writings sound a clarion call to their lawyer constituents to make the system work. They ask their peers to innovate, to be more honest, to work harder, do more pro bono work, make the public like lawyers, pull harder, bail faster, and be less adversarial—in an adversarial system. This exercise reminds me of that bromide about changing deck chairs on the *Titanic*. What they never say are those terrible words: "It ain't working, and it ain't gonna work. We must fundamentally change the American legal system."

Instead, they undertake futile public-relations campaigns to image the legal profession and its good works. Their public relations divisions mimic the scene in the Emerald City as they pin integrity, goodwill and public service on the legal profession much as the Wizard of Oz pinned a heart on the Tin Man and a medal on the Cowardly Lion and presented a diploma to the brainless Scarecrow.

A cursory examination of lawyer publications will reveal articles on lawyer-client, lawyer-public relations, and programs to improve lawyer images. There are afloat *pro bono* (free) legal services for those in our society who cannot afford legal representation in civil matters. Most overworked lawyers rightfully reject the bar association's attempt to require lawyers to give free time and opt for voluntary pro bono services if any.

The problem is that the whole exercise of imaging and free legal services for civil matters is doomed to failure. This has nothing to do with the good will of lawyers or the lack thereof. It relates to the theme of this book. The adversarial jury system of practice in America will ensure the demise of any program that does not address our fundamental system of law.

The businessperson who has just spent $5000 to win a verdict of $3000 which is uncollectible is not going to be made happy by public relations or attorney good will. It is even worse if the businessperson lost because the opposing side was able to convince the trier of fact of things that were simply not true.

The various American bar associations' search for an image of purity of purpose for their members is utterly futile. A high-minded image will forever elude the lawyer who labors in a legal system that places a premium on illusion and deception in its trial courts.

If America's trial lawyers want to seek a better image before the public, they must first re-examine the legal system itself. Trial lawyers should be counselors and problem solvers, not warriors. The adversarial system is too expensive and does not work adequately for most citizens. The bar associations would better serve their constituents and the public by returning to their original noble purposes and by replacing the legal system. Rather than lawyers performing pro bono work for the poor, why not create a legal system the poor can afford to use?

NOTES:

1. *The Petition of the Florida Bar Ass'n et. al., 40 So. 2nd 902, Supreme Court of Florida, en Banc, 7 June 1949.*

PART III

STRUCTURE AND PROCEDURE

CHAPTER XI

COURT STRUCTURE

For our purposes, a very general picture of the court systems of the United States will suffice.

There are two separate but often overlapping court systems. The federal court system, our national system, has *jurisdiction* (legal authority and power) in all fifty states and our possessions and territories.

Additionally, each state has its own court system, which has jurisdiction over state laws and the territory of the state and some concurrent jurisdiction with the federal system.

With some variation, the structure of the federal and state court systems and their functions are very similar and can be reduced to some simple generalizations. The federal system is set up like this:

United States Supreme Court: Final appeal court, nine judges;

United States Appeals Court: Appeal court, three or more judges; and

United States District Court: Trial court, single judge.

Let us start with the United States District Courts. These are the trial courts where jury and non-jury trials are conducted.

District courts have jurisdiction over violations of United States criminal laws, both *misdemeanors* (minor crimes) and *felonies* (major crimes) and over major civil matters involving citizens from different states.

For example, if a person is indicted (charged with a crime) for the violation of a federal law, such as tax evasion or robbing a post office, or is involved in a federal civil suit, the case is tried by a jury, or if the person waives a jury trial, by a judge in the United States District Court. This is the federal trial court.

A person who loses, or is unsatisfied with the results in the district court, may appeal to the United States Court of Appeals. There is no trial in the appeals court. On appeal, the appellant (the person who files the appeal) is restricted to arguing issues at law and not rehashing the facts. The argument is before a panel of judges. For example: The defendant is convicted of kidnapping, a violation of federal law. Prior to or at trial, the judge denied a motion to suppress some evidence and the defendant contends the judge made a legal mistake. The defendant then appeals to the United States Court of Appeals, asking the panel of judges to review and overturn the trial judge's decision. There are some exceptions to the strictly legal arguments before appellate courts, but they are not important for our discussion. The thing to remember is that there is no retrial of the facts in the appeal courts.

An appellant who is unsuccessful or loses again in the United States Court of Appeals may petition or ask the Supreme Court of the United States to hear the appeal at the highest level. If the question on appeal is important enough, the Supreme Court will hear the case. There is no right to appeal to the Supreme Court. The Supreme Court decides which cases it wants to review and actually listens to very few of the thousands it is requested to review. The state court systems mirror the federal system. The structure of the Florida court system, for example, looks like this:

Florida Supreme Court: Final appeal court, seven judges;

Florida District Court of Appeals: Appeal court, three or more judges;

Florida Circuit Court: Senior trial court, single judge; and

Florida County Court: Inferior trial court, single judge.

This system looks and works much like the federal system. As the problem is in the federal trial courts, not the appellate courts, so it is with the state courts. The problem lies in the circuit and county trial courts.

The circuit court has jurisdiction over felonies (crimes that carry sentences of more than one year in jail), civil suits involving large amounts of money, divorce, and other major matters. The county courts have jurisdiction over misdemeanors (crimes with a maximum sentence of one year or less in jail) and civil suits involving smaller amounts of money.

In short, that is the structure of all state court systems except that they are called different things in different states: county courts, justice-of-the-peace courts, division courts, department courts, city courts, magistrate courts, a whole profusion of names.

Encompassed in these trial courts are specialty courts that are attached to either the circuit courts or the county courts. They are traffic courts, juvenile courts, small-claims courts, dispute courts, and other subdivisions.

In these trial courts, not the appellate courts, lie the problems in the American legal system, the problems that are the focus of this book.

CHAPTER XII

LAW AND PROCEDURE

To understand the operation of the trial courts, the reader needs to recognize two types of law: substantive law and procedural law. These two types of law are dependent upon each other. Every other type of law—common law, code law, canon law, etc.—will fit under the umbrella of either substantive law or procedural law.

Substantive laws are passed by legislative bodies such as the United States Congress or the several state legislatures. They are the rules of our society, and they regulate our day-to-day conduct. Substantive laws are the laws against murder, laws regulating dissolution of marriage, laws defining our commercial relationships such as banking and contracts, and laws establishing our tax rates. There are thousands of these laws. All members of our society are presumed to know all these rules of our society—a major fiction.

The second type of law is *procedural law,* or as it is often called, "the rules of court." These rules tell lawyers how to file suit and how to proceed in the courtroom. There are both civil procedural rules and criminal procedural rules plus sub-categories of civil rules: for instance, bankruptcy, small claims, and guardianship. Substantive laws are enforced and applied in the trial courts by use of the procedural laws. Occasionally they conflict, but these conflicts are technicalities.

When the court system of the United States began to show signs of stress in the late 1930s, the Supreme Court of the United States worked to simplify the procedural rules. This process trickled down to the state courts, which also changed from a very technical and cumbersome type of pleading called common-law pleading to the less-technical system, the federal rules. This simplification of procedural law greatly improved the American court systems and allowed them to function fairly well for another thirty years.

We have evolved from an agricultural civilization to an industrial civilization into a communication civilization. With evolution, this agricultural-era court system has again become stressed, and the procedural-law changes made in the last fifty years have lost their medicinal value.

The courts, legislatures, and lawyer associations at both state and federal levels recognize that there are problems in our courts and are constantly casting about for solutions. Few, if any, of these seekers are considering a fundamental change to the entire American legal system; instead, they are constantly patching up the system. The patchwork has met with some short-term success but mainly long-term failure. For example: The legislatures have passed minimum mandatory sentences to address the crime problem. This has overloaded our prisons with a host of non-violent offenders and flooded our streets with child molesters, robbers, rapists, and other dangerous criminals.

Even if the legislative assemblies of the states and the United States Congress keep adjusting the system by adding more substantive laws, the system is so dysfunctional that it will still not work. The courts cannot do much more with the procedural rules; they are already fairly simple. They can be touched up here and there, but procedural adjustments will still not solve the problem. It makes little difference what adjustments are made to this antiquated system; it still will not work. The only solution is to replace the entire adversarial jury-trial system.

CHAPTER XIII

QUESTIONS OF EVIDENCE

The laws or rules of evidence are substantive laws that grew from court decisions about proceedings. Evidence rules are a sort of hybrid that determine what testimony or exhibits the trier of fact can consider, and they also tell the court how to proceed. I refer to them as the rules of evidence although many state legislatures have made them into quasi-substantive laws by passing bills that place them in the statute books. By codifying them, the legislatures have taken much of the rule-making function away from their judges concerning the admissibility of evidence. The rules of evidence do one of two things: they either allow the admission of evidence before the judge or jury, or they prevent the admission of evidence. For example: Florida Rule of Evidence 90.402 states, "All relevant evidence is admissible, except as provided by law." Rule 90.401 defines relevant evidence as ". . . evidence tending to prove or disprove a material fact." In a criminal trial, identification of the defendant as the one who committed the crime is relevant evidence. The prosecutor could present witnesses to testify they saw the defendant commit the crime.

The lawyer's goal in a trial is to bring all of his good

information (relevant evidence) before the trier of fact, whether it be judge or jury, and to exclude all the bad information (irrelevant evidence). He must do so playing by the rules of evidence. All information that is relevant is admissible unless the evidence can or should be excluded by using one of the other rules. Pursuant to Florida Rules of Evidence 90.404, character evidence is not admissible to prove that a person, usually the defendant in a criminal prosecution, acted in conformity with that particular trait. In theory, the rule prevents the inference that since the defendant committed some crime in the past, he must be guilty now. However, the prosecutor may present character evidence to prove a material fact, such as motive, opportunity, intent, preparation, or identity, but not solely to prove bad character. For example: If a defendant, whom none of the witnesses can identify because he always wore a mask, committed a string of crimes in a particular manner in the past, the prosecutor can present that evidence to show a mode of operation if the crime for which the defendant is being tried was committed in that same manner. The prosecutor may not present evidence that the defendant has six drunk-driving convictions if he is being tried for bank robbery.

Only information fairly procured and correctly presented is admissible to the jury. In theory this ensures fairness. The lawyer's job is to present his admissible evidence and stop the other lawyer from admitting his evidence.

Making the adversarial system worse is what is known as the "Exclusionary Rule." Simply stated: If the law-enforcement authorities obtain evidence by violating a criminal defendant's constitutional rights, the evidence may not be introduced by the prosecutor for the purposes of proving the defendant's guilt. The evidence will be excluded at the trial for criminal prosecution. If the unconstitutionally procured evidence leads to other evidence, that evidence may also be excluded based on what is called the "fruit of the poisonous tree" theory. The idea is to protect the citizen's constitutional rights and keep the cops honest. The result is frequently just the opposite. The exclusion allows many criminals back on the streets who then again violate the law-abiding citizen's rights by committing more crimes. The cops, realizing that to err is to let a criminal beat the system, simply lie about how they obtained the evidence. This rule creates bitter adversity between the lawyers and the witnesses in addition to the normal adversity between the lawyers.

Now we have the convoluted situation of the defendants, the "bad guys," telling the truth about an illegal search, and the cops, the "good guys," lying and committing perjury from the witness stand to get a conviction. The judges know the cops are lying, and the cops know they are taking a very small chance of being caught. Things are so bad that defense attorneys expect the cops to be lying somewhere in every major criminal case. Think about it: The cops who conducted an illegal search are not castigated by the court; the criminal goes free to prey on society; society, which is entitled to protection, is victimized again. In most criminal trials the clerks could forgo swearing witnesses to tell the truth and swear everybody to tell lies and it would make little difference. The juries would be more properly oriented deciding which witnesses were telling the fewest lies. It took two centuries and considerable genius to evolve a system this bad. Career criminals understand and have come to accept this goofy system and use it to their advantage.

Attorneys have the occasional opportunity to represent an innocent citizen who gets caught in this circus. The citizen's rights have been violated; he or she did not do it, but has been arrested and is in trouble. The citizen is stunned with the recognition that the boys in blue are trying to lie him into prison, and his attorney is amused at the citizen's naivete. The dismal part is that the cops are put in the position of having to lie in the first place. From the public's point of view, lying is an extremely bad habit for law-enforcement people to develop. Can we do anything to prevent this from happening? The way case law has developed, the solution may require a constitutional amendment. If law enforcement is violating citizens' constitutional rights, thereby violating the law, we need to penalize the violators, not protect the criminal at the expense of our civilization.

In the civil system, the rules of evidence that were designed to ensure fairness are more frequently used to hide the truth rather than to seek it. In the adversary atmosphere, one of the lawyers may be successful in suppressing his opponent's otherwise admissible evidence by clever use of the rules, thereby defeating the search for truth and reaching an unjust result. If one lawyer can deceive the judge by being brighter, better prepared, or dishonest, the system fails as does the search for truth and justice.

The natural response: If one lawyer has better prepared his case or is more knowledgeable, he should prevail. This underscores one point I am trying to make. The courtroom is too often a stage for lawyers to strut their skills of deception and put on a show rather than a problem-solving arena. Certainly it is not the touted institution wherein the litigants search for truth. Trials are contests to be won.

I recall a trial in which technique and rules completely dominated to the total exclusion of the merits of the case. My client sued a boat dealer for breach of warranty over a motor yacht he had purchased. The documents to prove purchase, repairs, requests, denials, etc., were voluminous. At a pre-trial conference between attorneys, defense counsel (my adversary) agreed that the 200-plus documents I showed to him were all relevant, and to save time, I could place the whole bunch into evidence as Plaintiff's Composite-Exhibit 1. Foolishly, I did not reduce our agreement to writing and have it entered as a pretrial order.

After the jury was selected and my first witness was seated in the witness box, I presented my packet of 200-plus documents to be admitted into evidence and received an unexpected objection from the defense. I argued to the judge our pre-trial oral agreement, but since it had not been reduced to writing, my argument fell on unsympathetic ears. The judge sustained my opponent's objection and told me to abide by the rules. I had to put the documents into evidence one by one.

The defense lawyer hoped that I had relied on his representations, dismissed my witnesses, and would therefore be unable to identify my client's documents. This would have prevented me from placing the documents before the jury, and he would have won by a technicality rather than on the merits of his case.

Fortunately, I had been practicing long enough to blindly trust few lawyers I did not know well. My witnesses were available, so I began the laborious process of placing my documents into evidence. This took three days rather than the half day it would have had the judge overruled my adversary's objection.

There is a little dance lawyers go through that has always made me feel self-conscious. I liken it to a gooney-bird mating ritual.

The lawyer picks up his document and walks or struts to the clerk's desk. Depending on how imperiously the judge conducts himself, the lawyer may have to ask permission of the judge each time before walking anywhere in the courtroom, especially near the judge's bench. At the clerk's desk the document is marked plaintiff's exhibit 1, 2, or 3 as the case may be. After the document is marked, the lawyer then walks to the witness box and asks the witness if he can identify the document and if it relates to the case. Of course, this is after the lawyer asks the judge's permission again. Depending on the type of evidence, the lawyer then bops across to opposing counsel's table and allows him or her to ogle the document. After it is properly ogled, the proffering lawyer asks the judge to admit the document into evidence. If there is no objection, the document is admitted. If there is an objection, argument and maybe more questions or cross examination of the witness ensues. After the document is admitted into evidence, the witness can testify as to the contents, and it can be published to the jury. This can take hours if not days when there are a lot of documents. Such rituals are part of the reason the system is so cumbersome and backed up.

My client was the plaintiff, and after our case was completed, the defense lawyer called his first witness. I objected to the defense's calling any witness on the grounds that the defense lawyer had failed to list any witness on his pre-trial statement. The judge hesitated; he knew what sustaining my objection meant. Since the defendant listed no witnesses, the defense could not call any witnesses to present testimony, so for all intents and purposes, he could not defend. When the judge hesitated, I reminded him as strongly as permissible that he had held my feet to the technical fire for three days. After a few minutes the judge agreed with me and disallowed the defendant's witnesses. With no witnesses to establish a defense, the jury ruled in my client's favor with little deliberation.

Could my adversary have won without the technicality? Probably.

So what happened? And what is the point other than that the defense lawyer got what was coming to him? The defense lawyer had pulled an unethical stunt that backfired. He made a misrepresentation hoping to make my presentation impossible.

In turn, I looked to see if he had dotted all the technical i's and crossed all the technical t's; he had not. This exemplifies a breakdown of what the system was designed to do. My point is this: The parties did not receive a trial on the merits; they received a resolution on technicalities. The system did not work well. Who was right on the merits? I do not even remember; besides, right and wrong were not the issue. The courtroom game was what I was required to play, not search for the truth or solve a problem.

Versions of this scenario happen every day in thousands of cases across the country. If a person is courtroom bound, there is a good chance that the case will never be heard on the merits. Right and wrong are not necessarily relevant, and simple fairness does not always apply. That is wrong, and that is a bad system of justice.

PART IV

HOW TO FIX IT

Richard D. Sparkman

CHAPTER XIV
CIVIL NON-ADVERSARIAL PROCEEDINGS

To call the American system of justice static, rather than dynamic, is not accurate. The federal courts, the state courts, and even the county courts are constantly striving to make the legal system work better. A great deal of hard work and good intentions go into change. The problem is, the change is not properly directed.

We are repairing and replacing parts on a system that is worn out and requires a total overhaul. We need to replace the adversarial approach to trial practice with a non-adversarial approach, eliminate the right to trial by jury, and replace our single-judge system with a three-judge system.

Once this is understood, we must then face the profundities of revolution or evolution, and with this choice come the attendant risks incurred when changing a fundamental institution. Revolution is riskier and may not be politically possible until the efficacy of fundamental change can be demonstrated. This can be demonstrated by an initial approach that does not require a constitutional change.

The key change, from which all the others can be developed, is to transform the combative-adversarial approach in our trial courts to a problem-solving approach. In other words, litigants and their lawyers should be encouraged, at first, then later mandated to seek solutions to their problems or differences in a cooperative manner rather than a combative, contentious manner. This idea is not new; it is consistent with the present trend toward mediation and the bar associations' search for alternatives.

The courts of each state could add rules providing for non-adversarial proceedings on a voluntary basis, at first. (See Appendix II). If the non-adversarial proceedings work, which they will, the courts and legislatures could mandate non-adversarial proceedings.

With only minor changes in the rules, the attorney filing the lawsuit could request non-adversarial proceedings. If the opposing attorney did not enter a timely objection, the suit would proceed non-adversarially. Since non-adversarial proceedings would be voluntary, there should be no objection from any quarter.

The non-adversarial court would consist of three judges with the concurrence of two judges necessary to reach a decision. It is important that these be real judges, like the appellate judges, not community do-gooders or weekend warriors. I am not suggesting a change in the way judges are appointed or elected; we will just need more of them. The judges would hear all proceedings *en banc*, together.

The trial would be in two parts, a procedure that would eliminate surprises and lead to settlements. This should be a real two-part trial, not a preliminary proceeding followed by the real trial.

At the commencement of the first trial, the attorneys would make informal opening statements to the judges. The parties, with advice of their attorneys and the court's consent, might be allowed to make personal opening statements. The court would be informed by counsel if there are emotions and anger involved and the reasons for the emotion and anger. This would give the court a total view of the problem, and it could take into consideration testimony whose source is anger or emotion.

The parties would then call witnesses who would be questioned by the judges and could be allowed to make statements at the pleasure of the court. The judges, being the searchers for truth, would control the proceedings and the questioning with the assistance of the attorneys. They would decide what evidence to hear and what, in fairness, must be excluded. The rules of evidence would be liberally construed to seek a just result. The attorney's role would be that of counselor and advisor, not movie star and deceiver as in our present system.

After all the witnesses have been heard and the evidence examined, the judges, attorneys, and litigants would enter an informal discussion to seek a solution. If a solution or compromise is not possible, each judge would, on the record, tell the parties and their attorneys his or her thinking and inclinations. Knowing the judges' thoughts would enable the parties to better prepare for the second trial. The trial would then be adjourned with a definite time set for the second trial. Having a time certain would be a godsend to the parties; the attorneys and witnesses would no longer have to guess when to take time from work or make travel plans.

Between the first and second trials, the parties would be able to seek new evidence, correct their mistakes, and adjust their thinking. This would eliminate the trial-by-ambush inherent in our present adversarial system. Being able to improve or even unable to improve one's position between trials and knowing the judges' inclinations would lead to more settlements before the second trial.

At the second trial, the judges would hear new evidence or changed positions. At the close of testimony, the judges would hear the law of the case as presented by the attorneys. If the parties could still not reach a settlement, the court would retire to deliberate in private, much like a jury, then return and render a decision.

A rules provision for non-adversarial proceedings can be either effected by legislative action or executed by the several supreme courts amending the rules of procedure. This most fundamental change does not appear to require any amendments to the Constitution. This latter point is extremely important. With no constitutional amendment required and no legislative action required, the most fundamental change in the American legal system in our history can be initiated by the courts themselves with only an after-the-fact veto power residing in the legislatures.

By adding a rule providing for non-adversarial proceedings, we take the first step on a journey to change from an adversarial system to a problem-solving system. There is nothing earth-shaking about this step. No one need be traumatized except those who fear the destination.

This type of non-adversarial proceeding will eliminate not only the adversarial problem, but the jury problem, the single-judge problem, and the mischief created by the rules of evidence. We cannot afford to reject trying this method, at least on an experimental basis.

This rule addition is easily instituted; and if it does not work, it is easily deleted. As an observer of non-adversarial problem-resolving methods, such as mediation, I know it will work because this method solves more than eighty per cent of the cases so treated without the authority of the court.

If the judges exercise their authority to speed up discovery procedures and motion practice, the whole court system will become more efficient. If the court system becomes more efficient, it will also be less expensive. Lower cost means better access for the working people of this country who are presently prone to abandon their $2000 or $3000 claim against the big guy.

At first the non-adversarial trials will be optional. The old system will still be available on demand so that opponents cannot attack this change with the argument that their rights are being whittled away. As the success of the non-adversarial system grows, jury-trial litigation will go the way of the dinosaur. It will, of course, be easier to determine who wants to use the court system for delay. It will become obvious that those who continue to seek jury trials in inappropriate situations are merely seeking to delay.

As the non-adversarial procedure matures and becomes accepted, it will then be possible to amend the constitutitions to entirely eliminate the adversarial-jury system.

This kind of trial can also help to unburden our appeals courts. Those who settle voluntarily will waive any appeal. Since the rules are simple and admission of evidence is liberal, there will be few judicial errors to be appealed. Most appeals involve alleged questions of error concerning procedure and evidence rather than questions concerning facts.

The most important benefit to our citizens that will be derived from the concept of the non-adversarial proceedings I am advocating will be the choice of *self-representation*. With minimal help in preparing pleadings, every citizen will at least have the opportunity to present his or her case in court. Accepting and implementing this courtroom concept will, for the first time, give Americans a true democratic court system.

Non-adversarial dispute resolution will be of inestimable social value to our society. Daily, our citizens leave our courtrooms in a state of rage. They are the subject of the next day's headlines. A non-adversarial legal system will go a long way toward that kinder and gentler society our Presidents promise us but fail to provide.

Richard D. Sparkman

CHAPTER XV

CRIMINAL NON-ADVERSARIAL PROCEEDINGS AND THE CONSTITUTIONAL PROBLEM

The most difficult to change will be the criminal-justice system because of the constitutional problem. Trial by jury is indeed guaranteed by the United States Constitution. The Supreme Court's interpretations of citizens' rights in the Bill of Rights have given us the exclusionary rules. Fundamental changes in the criminal-justice system will require constitutional amendments. We could, however, test the efficacy of voluntary non-adversarial criminal proceedings.

Voluntary non-adversarial proceedings similar to the civil proceedings discussed in Chapter XIV will not be offensive to either the United States Constitution or to the constitutions of the states.

A citizen is at liberty to waive most of his or her constitutional rights such as trial by jury, prohibition of a warrantless search, or even refusal to be a witness against one's self. Providing for non-adversarial trials before a three-judge court as an elective will not deny our citizens any of the constitutional protections at either the state or federal level.

There is no reason the same format as suggested for civil trials cannot be used for criminal trials. If the accused knowingly and voluntarily waived trial by jury and adversarial proceedings, he or she could have an informal trial before a three-judge panel.

A criminal defendant who is guilty with a reasonable explanation would have a tremendous advantage by electing to proceed through the proposed non-adversarial system. The defendant's explanation could be a part of the trial, which is precluded until sentencing in our present adversarial trials. Non-adversarial trials could be even more socially effective and desirable if the legislatures would untie the judges' hands by eliminating minimum mandatory sentences. In Everglades City, Florida, a substantial part of the community began hauling marijuana in their boats as a result of a decline in the fishing industry because of environmental problems and laws closing fishing grounds. These were not mean, terrible people; they were ordinary fishermen trying to feed their children with no source of income. I have listened to many judges apologize to the defendants for the inappropriate sentence they were required to impose. In the Everglades case, our country unnecessarily locked up a large portion of a very fine community of non-violent citizens for a very long time because of the lack of flexibility in the legal system. In a non-adversarial criminal trial, fad crimes like the Everglades example in which adversarial prosecutors can enrage juries will be put into their proper perspective.

Innocent defendants with weak defenses will have the opportunity to explain informally the reason for their dilemma.

This is something not so easily accomplished in the more formal adversarial courtroom. I believe this sort of innocent defendant stands a much better chance before three judges than before a jury when there are heightened emotions. Prosecutors use emotion to enrage juries to ensure convictions. A prosecutor once told me it was more fun to convict an innocent person. It demonstrated prosecutorial prowess in the adversarial system.

Prosecutors will find it very difficult to goad judges into emotional rulings. I have always tried to avoid jury trials in cases that contain a lot of highly emotional or shocking testimony. A rule change to test voluntary non-adversarial criminal proceeding is easily instituted. If it does not work, it is easily deleted. Since we have trial by brokerage anyway, this will not change things much except to help the innocent and protect defendants involved in emotion-generating crimes that carry minimum mandatory sentences.

Constitutional-protection issues will arise only when we decide to mandate non-adversarial proceedings or to eliminate the right to trial by jury entirely. In fact, it may not be politically possible to completely eliminate trial by jury. At least it will not be politically possible until the citizens of America see the efficacy of the system I am proposing.

Once we test the three-judge, non-adversarial trial and it becomes standard practice in our courtrooms, we will stand a better chance to amend our constitutions. I believe it will then be politically possible to eliminate trial by jury in all cases but those dealing with the most heinous crimes.

Maintaining the right to jury trial in capital cases will make amending the state and federal constitutions much easier than if we try to eliminate juries altogether. And maybe we should keep a remnant of the American adversarial jury-trial system around to provide amusement and to remind us just how horrible it was. We are now so accustomed to these dog-and-pony shows, however, that they have lost much of their entertainment value.

If it remains politically impossible to limit trial by jury, there is another way to make jury trials almost as effective as non-adversarial three-judge trials yet considerably more undesirable. We can give jurors the right to question witnesses and to direct the proceedings much as grand juries do today. That should raise the hair on the back of the neck of even the most hardened criminal.

Present-day juries sit like bumps on logs and are spoon-fed the testimony and evidence the attorneys want them to hear. I have seen few jury trials in which the jurors were satisfied with the information they took to the jury room. They inevitably ask the judge for additional evidence and clarifications only to be denied because the evidence phase of the trial is closed.

A criminal defendant or a crooked business person involved in a case before a jury that could take over the questioning role presently reserved to lawyers and judges would be hard pressed to deceive the jury as is the norm in our contemporary courts. This procedure could be instituted without constitutional amendments. Nothing in any constitution says that juries must sit passively and be deceived. We have evolved to this state only by precedent.

If we can amend the constitutions of the states and of the United States to eliminate the jury system, America's crime rate will plummet. In a non-adversarial, non-jury trial system, criminals will have little chance of beating the system. The chances of deceiving three judges who may question witnesses at length will be substantially less than the chances of deceiving a jury. The criminal-justice system will become credible.

To America's juvenile delinquents the criminal-justice system is not credible. If we make the criminal-justice system credible, and the system I am advocating will be nothing if not credible, it will begin to serve as a deterrent.

It is axiomatic that once criminal defendants are through the technical stage of the proceedings and are finally faced with a jury, most develop cold feet and enter their pleas. Guilty criminals facing a three-judge trial court they know their lawyers cannot deceive will get colder feet much faster and speed up the criminal-justice system by entering pleas sooner. When the government must take a defendant through a full trial, a three-judge trial will be a lot faster and less cumbersome than a jury trial. We could hold more trials and eliminate the blackmail system of criminal justice.

A credible criminal-justice system backed by improved police techniques will take America closer to a solution to her crime problem. A better handle on crime will have a beneficial effect on every sector of our society from tourism to the price of retail merchandise.

Changing to a better legal system requires only the understanding of what needs to be done and why we should do it, and the will to get on with the job.

CHAPTER XVI

THE CONSEQUENCES OF CHANGE

The role of lawyers will change dramatically in a non-adversarial, non-jury legal system. If we will need twice the number of judges, we will need substantially fewer lawyers.

Since lawyers will be counselors rather than warriors, those many fine lawyers who have avoided trial work because of its adversarial nature will drift into, or back to, the courtroom.

Today's trial lawyer spends tremendous time and energy trying to figure out how to beat the system or how to beat the opponent. In a non-adversarial system, the lawyer would concentrate on understanding his or her client's problem and trying to solve it in a way consistent with the laws rather than scheming to beat the system or an opponent.

The lawyer's job will be to counsel, conciliate, and solve problems or seek solutions. There will be no advantage in taking a bad case to court in hopes of deceiving the trier of fact sufficiently to win. The best lawyers will be those who are smart enough to quietly negotiate a superior position for their clients rather than the mellifluous-voiced actors.

Probably the biggest benefit to America's trial lawyers will be to give them an extension on life. It makes little difference how tough a lawyer is: trial work is terribly stressful. The stress is in not knowing when one is going to be blindsided or not being able to predict an unstable or inconsistent judge.

Young turks generally cannot wait to get into the trial arena and draw first blood; however, theirs is generally the first and most copiously drawn. The axiom that age and treachery will defeat youth and enthusiasm is truer in the courtroom than in any other theater. By the time a trial lawyer gets good enough to lower the stress level, he or she is ready to turn in the sword and be a counselor.

America will lose the lawyer of folklore, the great mouthpiece. Just as the ten-gallon hat will disappear with the metric system, the storied lawyer destroying the bad guy with withering cross examination will fall with the adversarial jury system. Both will go the way of the passenger pigeon, but unlike the passenger pigeon, good riddance. In fact, a non-adversarial system may put a few lawyers out of work. This will probably not traumatize the non-lawyer population. In any case, it is a small price to pay for a legal system that works.

Judges

America will need more judges but not as many as it may first appear. There will be fewer trials in a non-adversarial, non-jury system, and trials will be much faster without the laborious task of jury selection.

Since the courtroom burdens of examination and cross-examination will now fall to the judges, the judges who do not possess those skills will have to learn them. Solo judges will have to learn to work collegiately. A judge's role in the trial process will be considerably greater.

There is, on the other hand, safety in numbers. Many judges now lock themselves in fortress-like chambers, and not a few carry guns for self-protection. Those flamboyant judges, so loved by the public because they rant from the bench at the bad guys, will lose their stage and maybe their jobs. Again, good riddance: they are generally the least effective anyway.

The most superfluous words in America are spoken with authority and ostentation from the judge's perch. Go into America's courtrooms and listen to judges lecture convicted felons before they pronounce sentence. Listen to a judge lecture a felon on the proper way to live before pronouncing a life sentence or even a death sentence. I have never met a felon who could remember what the judge said during sentencing. Every one is in a state of shock. It is pure baloney for public consumption, and I wish they would stop.

If we cannot elect or appoint judges with enough brains to stop such nonsense, a three-judge system will tend to curtail this prattle. A single judge doing silly things just draws grimaces from the attorneys. Silliness exaggerated three times would draw such roils of laughter and derision that it would quickly cease. I never see the nonsense in an appeals court that I occasionally see in a single-judge trial court.

A three-judge court system can sandwich the really incapable judge and save our citizens a world of grief. The best-run system in America is a family-law court with an excellent judge. The worst-run system in America is a family court with a bad judge. No American citizen deserves the fate of standing before one bad judge. The least we can do for our citizens is to give them decent courts.

Personal Injury Cases

I cannot imagine a three-judge court allowing an injured person to walk away uncompensated by the wrongdoer. Seeing the attitude and conduct of a fair segment of corporate America toward those persons they have injured, or for whom they are responsible, is a saddening experience. It is a cliche that corporations have no conscience, but some of America's insurance companies have less than none. Some of them treat injury victims as enemies to be defeated.

An insurance company or a tort feasor that knows it must face the injured person in a credible personal-injury court will make speedy and reasonable settlements. It does not make settlements today because it knows it can pervert the personal-injury legal system with experts for hire.

This lack of credibility in our court system costs taxpayers millions for regulatory agencies to try to keep the few really irresponsible insurance companies in line. With a credible court system, the regulatory agencies could contract rather than expand every year.

It will be more economical for persons to bring their injuries before a reformed court. Victims who currently cannot afford to sue for compensation in our present system will have court access. Treating doctors, who are sick of being beaten up in our adversarial courts, will be more willing to testify for their patients for a reasonable fee. Those doctors who are professional insurance-company witnesses will quickly lose their credibility before a three-judge court. When judges hear professional witnesses testify in a series of cases, they will be in a better position to reject "testimony for hire" than the jurors who see the witness only once.

On the other hand, judges are not likely to award ridiculous sums for fad cases or because a gifted lawyer has outraged them over a unique factual situation. A reformed court system will level out personal-injury awards, reduce the cost of insurance, and turn the American legal system into a reasonable one as far as injured people are concerned.

Business

Changing to a non-adversarial, non-jury system will lift the legal yoke from the neck of American business. Under the present adversarial system, the business person wronged in a transaction must suffer interminable delays and navigate through a maze of legal proceedings until the case is before a trier of fact. When the businessperson arrives at court, if the case is still worth anything, he gets to see who has the better lawyer, not which case has merit.

The change I am advocating will unload the court system in short order because there will be little advantage in legal maneuvering and even less advantage in filing a nuisance or frivolous lawsuit.

A system like this will greatly reduce business-killing delays and virtually eliminate exorbitant product-liability awards. Most appropriate for business is the maxim, "Justice delayed is justice denied." A speedy system will give the dishonest business person less time to hide assets and the damaged party a better shot at recovery. Legal costs saved in business by a more economical legal system can be reinvested in business or passed on to the consumer.

As our economy becomes more international in scope, Americans are placed at a disadvantage by a legal system that cannot respond quickly enough to the needs of the business community.

Foreign business people who are wary of, and often dread the American legal system, will feel more comfortable about investing in American business. Too much of America's business ability and resources are eaten up in bickering and litigation for healthy competition in the world economy. The price of the failure to change is the failure to prosper in the world markets to the full extent of our economic capacity.

American business cannot afford to ignore nor fail to see that they will be one of the biggest winners in the change from an adversarial system to a non-adversarial system. From automobiles to tobacco to pharmaceuticals American business is, at any time, a prime target for a runaway verdict in an adversarial jury trial. All American manufactuers are well advised to sign onto this concept and fight diligently until America abandons the adversarial trial system.

I remind manufacturers that their very existence, faced with a lawsuit in our adversarial trial system, rests on the ability of their best lawyer.

Citizens

One of the primary contentions of this book is that the legal system is too expensive. It is too expensive because it is too complex. Citizens without legal training can rarely navigate their way through anything more complex than a simple small-claims case. To watch a person who is not legally trained try to pick a jury and deal with the technicalities of a trial is not amusing. Few of even our most intelligent citizens can do it. We may have a government of the people, by the people, and for the people; but we do not have a legal system of the people, by the people, and for the people.

We have developed a legal system that can be run only by lawyers. In many areas, only specialists can adequately perform. Lawyers cost too much because the cost of doing legal business is too high.

In a non-adversarial, non-jury system, most citizens will be competent to handle much of their legal business. When citizens have to hire attorneys, they will be affordable if they do not have to function in an ambush environment doing extra research and preparation to cover their posteriors.

If Americans want a legal system citizens can use, they are going to have to get rid of the present one.

CHAPTER XVII

PRIVATIZATION

If our judiciary, our lawyers, and our bar associations resist the sort of changes I am advocating in this book, the penalty will be severe. That penalty will be the privatization of the legal system. If it is unthinkable that an essential government institution can be privatized, ask the post office.

Privatization of the American legal system is underway apace at this minute. Private personal-injury mediation has been so successful in the last decade that it is now the personal-injury litigation method of choice by many lawyers and the more responsible insurance companies.

Two decades ago few personal-injury cases were negotiated by private mediators. Once the overloaded and stagnated courts started referring cases to mediation, the trend caught on. Lawyers started arranging mediation without court order and only memorialized their settlements with the courts. This is becoming common practice in personal-injury cases today.

Now the trend is to ignore the courts, mediate the problem without filing suit, then write contracts and settlements between the parties. Personal-injury claims are now handled routinely outside the judicial system. These are not just small-claims actions: these are major money claims presented to private mediators.

The same thing is happening in family disputes and divorces. At first the lawsuits were filed in the courts, then presented to mediators. Within the last few years, family dispute-resolution centers have sprung up, and they now mediate disputes before suits are filed. After a dispute is mediated, basic pleadings are filed in the courts to finalize and legalize the agreement.

I envision private franchised dispute centers or national dispute centers that will take over the gravy functions of the courts much as the parcel services took the gravy from the post office.

As a lawyer, I view the privatization of the legal system with mixed emotions. The private dispute centers work pretty much along the lines I am advocating to change the American legal system. They work, and they work far better than our government-sponsored legal system. But they also open the door to untrained persons in the practice of law. I do not favor untrained people making critical legal decisions for our citizens. I have seen the results of enough jailhouse advice and even poor legal advice to oppose the unlicensed practice of law. This, in addition to privatization, can lead to a decline in the viability of the bar and maybe endanger the very existence of the independent bar association.

The decline of an independent bar may not raise any red flags for a public amused by the current rash of lawyer jokes, but it should. The independent bar is the first and last line of defense against totalitarian elements or practices at any level of government. In government scandals there is always the cry for an independent counsel because of the counsel's very independence. If we lose the independent bar as a viable force in America, we will endanger our freedoms far more seriously than any reform in our legal system might do.

The bar associations of the several states should be in the vanguard to change our legal system to one that better serves our citizens. Failure to address their conservatism may well mean the death of these associations, which would leave our citizens subject to a law-enforcement establishment with few restraints. Anyone intelligent enough to read this far into the book knows the danger of even the best-meaning, unrestrained police force.

Richard D. Sparkman

CHAPTER XVIII

CAVEAT

There are elements of our legal system so valuable we dare not tamper with them. If to change is to lose these elements, I will be the first to discourage the changes I am advocating.

The most important element of the American legal system is access. In previous chapters I have criticized the American legal system because of its financial limits on total access for low-income and middle-income families. I now differentiate between the legal right to access and the financial ability to fully utilize that access. It is elementary that if a citizen has no legal access to a court or a judge, that citizen cannot obtain the protection of the courts. In America we have universal legal access to our courts. Anybody can file a lawsuit asking for any kind of relief on any subject. At least all our citizens and even aliens can get in the door of the courthouse. Meaningful access may stop inside the door, depending on financial resources, but at least a person can file the suit. This access is the most important feature of our legal system.

When arrested in America, the prisoner is taken before a magistrate or a judge without undue delay. In most states the prisoner is before the official within forty-eight hours and in many states within twenty-four hours. The certainty that one will not languish in a cell without hearing or access to the court is our most precious safeguard. In many countries, a prisoner can be locked in jail, incommunicado, indefinitely. Incarceration without communication is a most disspiriting and oppressive ordeal. That does not happen frequently in America, and for that we must be grateful.

At the first appearance, the prisoner experiences the second but equally most valuable procedure in the American legal system. The prisoner is given a date certain for the next appearance before the court. Without a date certain for a future appearance, the first appearance would be rendered meaningless.

Our universal access extends to all cases, both criminal and civil, before the many courts in our country. I cannot express how valuable such access is. To lose this access is to eschew all thoughts of reform. The changes I am advocating will not, however, endanger access to our courts; in fact, they will increase access. Once financial impediments to access are removed, theoretical universal access will change to real universal access.

An independent judiciary, controlled by neither the executive nor the legislature, is another essential element for the protection of our freedoms and the safeguarding of our rights. It is the key to the balance-of-powers concept we all learned in middle-school civics. There is nothing in the changes I am advocating that will endanger the independent judiciary.

Americans are rightly uncomfortable when any idea comes along that could adversely affect any right guaranteed by the Bill of Rights. The changes I am suggesting will directly affect the right of trial by jury. I am suggesting a constitutional amendment to eliminate trial by jury in all but capital cases. If we eliminate the death penalty, I suggest we completely abandon trial by jury. In a non-adversarial system there will be no advantage to having a jury, so juries will be merely time-consuming, costly dinosaurs.

The only reason we had juries to begin with was to give commoners a reasonable likelihood of fairness in courts run by the aristocracy. We do not have a nobility in America; all our judges are commoners—some very common. The rationale for jury trials was eliminated over two hundred years ago by the American Revolution.

The remainder of the Bill of Rights will not be directly affected by the changes I am advocating. There will be no direct effect on speedy trials, search-and-seizure prohibitions, bails, cruel and unusual punishment, or the basic rights we trial lawyers struggle daily to protect.

Therefore, I do not believe the changes I am advocating will in any manner endanger the privileges or immunities of the citizens of the United States. On the contrary, I believe these changes will make this country a safer, juster society.

Richard D. Sparkman

EPILOGUE

Man's most valuable tool, the word, is the tool of the lawyer and the tool used in the courtroom. With language, man learned to communicate, organize, cooperate, and solve problems. Adversity with a small "a" challenges, creates competition, engenders debate, and gives man the need to cooperate to solve problems. Adversity with a large "A," denoting hostility, contrariness, conflict, combat, the very essence of the adversarial-jury trial system in America, has more frequently led to dysfunction.

For the afficionados of struggle I offer the consolation that, at the very least, cooperation is less expensive than conflict.

That the American legal system is better than some other legal systems in the world does not mean it is a good system or as good as it could be. That justice cannot be bought and sold as a commodity in the market place, as it can in many third-world countries, does not mean justice is not indirectly for sale. The rich have always tried the poor, and the strong have always tried the weak. This is legitimate, because that is the way things have always been, the way things will remain, and the only way things can ever be. Even accepting the inevitable, however, we can strive to rebalance things a little.

Most Americans view the legal system from a distance, and it looks okay. It is only the veterans such as single parents, small-business persons, or folks with a fruitcake for a neighbor who know how ineffective and bad our legal system can be. I ask any citizen who doubts my contentions and recommendations to survey veterans of the American legal system.

We have a legal system that cannot control our criminals and a civil system that cannot provide for the equal protection of our citizens. We must move toward a new system of justice since we have not been able to fix the one we have. Simply understanding the problem brings us halfway to the solution. Instituting the rule changes that initially provide for voluntary non-adversarial proceedings will make evident the efficacy of cooperative problem solving to even the most ardent combatant. We can then address the problem of a jury system administered by single judges.

There is a great deal of movement in the direction of privatization. Mediation and other methods of dispute settlement are proliferating. Privatization of the court system is not a new idea; it is the articulation of a trend already underway and of an idea whose time has come.

Change cannot and will not be completed overnight. Scrambling about our courtrooms are several generations of lawyers trained in combat, and our law schools are pouring forth young turks who smell blood and thirst for this combat. This is okay; let them run riot for a while: we have already been doing it for more than two centuries. After they have financially wrecked and emotionally destroyed a sufficient number of their clients, they, too, will have matured and will seek an alternate method of practice.

The important thing is to understand and to begin our journey. By the beginning of the Twenty-first Century, we can put this legal beast in its cage and evolve a new system.

The path to change is understanding. When our legislators and the judiciary profoundly understand that America's four-hundred-year experiment with the adversarial jury system has failed, our leadership will consider another course.

If we fail to change, we run the high-end risk of destroying the independent bar associations, which could give us, if not a police state, the next thing to it. On the low-risk side, our citizens will continue to suffer injustices, and our business people will be handicapped in the world markets. The American legal system is going to get worse before it gets better, so it is time to act.

We need a legal system that provides meaningful access to all our citizens, not just those who can afford to hire lawyers. We need, and will always have, a legal system; we may as well have a good one.

Richard D. Sparkman

APPENDIX I

The trial of all crimes, except in cases of impeachment, shall be by jury, and such trial shall be held in the state where the said crimes shall have been committed; but when not committed within any state the trial shall be at such place or places as the Congress may by law have directed.

Constitution of the United States
Article III. Section 2 (3).

In all criminal prosecutions, the accused shall enjoy the right to a speedy and public trial, by an impartial jury of the State and district wherein the crime shall have been committed, which districts shall have been previously ascertained by law, and to be informed of the nature and cause of the accusation; to be confronted with the witnesses against him; to have compulsory process for obtaining witnesses in his favor, and to have the assistance of counsel for his defense.

Amendments to the Constitution of the United States
Article VI

In suits at common law, where the value in controversy shall exceed twenty dollars, the right of trial by jury shall be preserved, and no fact tried by a jury shall be otherwise re-examined in any court of the United States than according to the rules of the common law.

Amendments to the Constitution of the United States Article VII

APPENDIX II

Non-Adversarial Proceedings

RULE 1 A party may endorse upon a pleading a request for non-adversarial proceedings. If the opposing party does not demand trial by jury or non-jury adversarial proceedings, the action shall be tried non-adversarially.

COMMENT: At the beginning of a lawsuit, the filing lawyer can elect this new method of trial. If the responding attorneys agree, the action is tried non-adversarially. This is voluntary, therefore not offensive to the Constitution.

RULE 1.1 Non-Adversarial Trials

(a) Three judges shall constitute the trial court in non-adversarial proceedings. Concurrence of two judges shall be necessary to a decision.

COMMENT: Three judges are common in appeals courts and have been seen in extraordinary proceedings in trial courts. We will need more judges, but the efficacy of the system will require fewer lawyers, which should be a relief to the population.

(b) Trial shall be bifurcated and shall proceed as follows:

(1) The parties shall proffer an opening statement of the case, identifying the issues and witnesses, outlining the expected testimony and making a request for relief.

(2) The judges shall question the parties and witnesses.

(3) The lawyers shall counsel their clients and may request and suggest interrogatories by the judges.

COMMENT: The lawyers' job is to seek an advantageous solution for their clients. The judges' job is to seek the truth and a fair solution. It makes sense to have the seekers of truth control the evidence and the course of proceedings. The judges are not out to hide anything.

(4) All relevant evidence shall be admissible. Inadmissible evidence may be proffered.

COMMENT: The judges will be able to hear the evidence they need to hear. This liberal admission of evidence is already customary in administrative proceedings.

(5) At the close of evidence, the parties and the court will enter into an informal discussion to seek a solution. The judges shall each convey to the parties their thinking.

COMMENT: The parties will, during the proceedings, gain an idea of where they stand with the court and adjust their thinking and proceedings accordingly. They do not have to study the judges' expressions and guess their positions; they will be told. In the present system, the judges sit like sphinxes and deliver the prize or the blow at the end, often a surprise to everyone. We do not need trial decisions by surprise; we need solutions.

(6) If no solution is reached, the trial shall be adjourned to reconvene at a date certain, not to exceed twenty days except for extraordinary circumstances stated on the record.

COMMENT: No one ever tried a perfect case: something is always forgotten; witnesses are frequently unavailable. The parties will have time to correct their mistakes, supplement their positions, and rethink their options.

(7) Upon reconvening the trial, the judges shall hear additional testimony and consider new positions. The judges shall again encourage settlement.

(8) If the parties cannot settle, the judges shall render a decision.

COMMENT: The parties will have had every opportunity to settle their cases, thereby obviating appeals.

Richard D. Sparkman

APPENDIX III

FURTHER COMMENTS

I received many lecture opportunities and a host of mail following the release of the first edition of *FAILED JUSTICE*. This mail and the audiences focused their comments on several subject areas. Foremost were discussions considering new ways to run our trials, within the adversarial system. Suggestions ranged from the use of professional juries to substituting lay judges for lawyer-judges to allowing juries to ask occasional questions. Most of these persons missed the point. All of these solutions struggled with the same dysfunctional adversarial system and proffered plans to make it work.

I ask these persons to reflect on their thinking. The bar associations of this country have a host of committees and subcommittees laboring tirelessly year after year to find ways to make the adversarial system work efficiently. They have labored thus for decades. These extremely intelligent and dedicated people have failed. They have simply been unable to make America's trial systems control our criminals, provide equal protection through the laws, or provide cost-effective legal services. They are so far from reaching even one of these goals that it only amazes me that thousands of intelligent, well-educated people will labor at failure so assiduously.

I feel I must repeat myself on the potential of our adversarial jury-trial system. "It ain't working, and it ain't gonna work."

There is only one way, my fellow citizens: Scrap the adversarial trial system and replace it with a non-adversarial system. If we do not make this change, all reform is in vain.

Our four-hundred-year experiment with the adversarial jury system has failed. I leave you with one further thought on this subject. We have an entire professional class, criminal-trial lawyers, whose job is to make sure that drunk drivers are returned to our streets, drug dealers are free to sell to our children, and killers are free to prey again. As a trial lawyer, I have personally accomplished each of these goals. If a helicopter is a machine struggling to tear itself to pieces, any society that has an adversarial jury-trial system is a society bent on self-destruction. We are beginning to self-destruct.

The second subject area revealed such a frustration with the system that it has spawned a desire to weaken or destroy its officers. More than one person railed at the power and maliciousness of judges and lawyers. These persons universally viewed lawyers as diabolical and judges as satanic abusers of power. These alienated citizens suggested taking power away from the legally trained and returning it to the people. Not one was able to explain exactly what returning power to the people means. Their ideas ranged from ill-designed schemes of citizen courts to vigilantism to anarchy.

It seemed impossible to convince these people that lawyers and judges are, by and large, a rather normal group of well-intended people stuck in a dysfunctional legal system that they can neither control nor know how to fix. That lawyer institutions do nothing about the fundamental failures of the adversarial system probably has more to do with inertia and the consevativeness of bureaucracies than with malevolence.

I personally know many lawyers. I can count on one hand those I could label demonic. It takes a calculator to count the honest ones. Simply stated, those persons who blame the failures of the American trial system on the maliciousness of lawyers and judges are wrong.

That power must be exercised is axiomatic in any civilization. That the judicial power of the United States rests in the hands of a conscientious group of human beings is a fact. That judicial power is occasionally abused is a reality. If we killed all the lawyers and replaced them with other sorts of persons or class of citizens, our system would not work one bit better and probably a lot worse.

I invite these well-intended citizens to refocus their thinking from an error, the invidiousness of lawyers, to the real problem, our dysfunctional adversarial-jury system. To counsel political alienation is to flirt with real danger. We will scrap the adversarial system or our streets will be controlled by thugs and eventually our parliaments will be controlled by the product of thugs.

In other words, there is no real choice. If we do not replace the adversarial system, we will build a police state or we will suffer varying degrees of anarchy and dissolution.

If anyone would like to contact the author to further discuss the concepts in this book, or to comment in any way, please feel free to do so at the following address:

Richard D. Sparkman
Sparkman & Quinn
P.O. Box 7128
Naples, FL 34101

Your comments and observations will be greatly appreciated.

Richard D. Sparkman

APPPENDIX IV

HOW TO ACCOMPLISH CHANGE

The most frequent question at my lectures was prefaced with the comment that I was understood and that the questioner agreed with me, but to fundamentally change the system was an impossible dream: how would it ever be done? Cited were the history of the system, its vested interests, and the real or perceived constitutional problems.

My response was to discuss the inevitability of change and the absolute necessity that the change be along the lines I am advocating. That the system changes every year is axiomatic. That those changes do not solve the greater problem is obvious.

If we do not now have a national crisis on out streets, we are fast apporaching one. There appears nothing in our public policies or on the legislative agenda of any political party that will derail the freight train of disorder. Our streets are peopled with ever-growing gangs of predatory and homicidally violent criminals, and the alienated folks are arming themselves to the teeth for confrontation.

There is but one solution: new thinking to change our court system to a non-adversarial system.

This change can be relatively simple, inexpensive, and quick if those who understand its absolute necessity follow two simple and easy courses of action.

First, we must convince the persuasive portion of our population and our legislative and judicial leadership of two fundamental concepts. The first is that our present system is not working and that change is possible under our Constitution.

How difficult can this be? It is self-evident to all but the least aware of our citizens that our present system is not working as we expect or hope it will work. It may take a few minutes to explain why it never will, but after the explanation, only those in emotional denial can resist fundamental change.

The second course, is also not very difficult. Concerned citizens must read <u>Failed Justice</u> and pass it to their fellow citizens to read. Then we must send <u>Failed Justice</u> to our legislators and the judiciary with strong exhortations that they read and study these concepts. These leaders will then initiate a national debate; and, when all is said and done, it will be manifest that one reasonable solution is the solution proposed in <u>Failed Justice</u>.

I emphasize that we cannot depend on "George" to do it. Each concerned citizen must send his or her copy of <u>Failed Justice</u> to the authorities. One book on a legislator's desk is unimp[ressive. A bombardment with the same book will be taken seriously.

AFTERWORD

A nation that will not control its criminals will eventually be controlled by criminals.

Along with many of my fellow citizens, I perceive a moral decline in America, albeit a different and far more insidious decline than that of our frequently faulted sexual mores.

America's uninspired approach to drug addiction has loaded our prison with addicts and so mixed them with real criminals that it is difficult to distinguish between really bad folks and addicts. As a result, the friends, relatives, and acquaintances of those imprisoned addicts no longer attach shame to conviction and imprisonment. In many inner-city ghettos young men all expect to go to prison, sooner or later, and for some it is a career path.

Federal penitentiaries that cater to white collar criminals are known as "country clubs." Once a person has "done his time" rights are restored, almost as a matter of course, and the person goes forth as a cleansed soul. Crimes and wrongdoing are something to get away with rather than a public disgrace. As a moral standard, this can be a nation killer if not a civilization killer.

It is unacceptable that technological America will not control its criminals and it is appalling that there is no longer a stigma to being convicted of a criminal offense. This unwillingness to control our criminals and the acceptance of bad people as just making a mistake is our real moral dilemma.

If <u>Failed Justice</u> has taught us anything, it is that our trial system will never control our criminals and we will continue our moral decline until we scrap this system and build a new one. In our civil courts the honest citizen stands little chance against the dishonest litigant who lies with impunity.

There is no choice: building a decent trial system is a prerequisite to solving our crime problem, and solving our crime problem is fundamental to putting our civilization's house in order. If we do not successfully address the fundamentals, the Twenty-first Century will be Europe's or Asia's century and not America's century. The world will have lost the moral leadership that has taken it to the brink of world democracy. With that leadership gone, the future is ever more uncertain.

I am told that man is only three days from barbarism. After the first day without food, a man will lie for it; after the second, he will steal it; after the third, he will kill for it. I suggest that a civilization in distress from internal problems is only one coup from totalitarianism.

Might the tide, for the United States, be running out, and is a new dark age clouding the horizon? It is not inconceivable. If we are unwilling to address these fundamental problems, maybe Europe or Asia will save civilization; we certainly will not.

THE CRIMINAL'S CONFEDERATE
(ANONYMITY)

BY
RICHARD D. SPARKMAN

In the year of our Lord one thousand nine hundred and ninety eight or thereabouts, look for a new book by Richard D. Sparkman, The Criminal's Confederate (Anonymity).

Sparkman, who has practiced trial law for twenty five years, knows the criminal and how the criminal functions. Knowing criminals and talking to them daily for over two decades, Sparkman knows what makes them tick.

Using a format similar to Failed Justice, Sparkman explains how or why a criminal is successful and why he is occasionally unsuccessful.

More important, The Author tells America how to reduce her crime rate by up to 60% in less than a decade without building a police state or ripping up the Constitution.

As with most great solutions, his is rather simple and easily implemented.

Contact: Eastlery Publishing
           307 Airport Rd. N.
           Naples, Fl. 34104

Richard D. Sparkman

For additional copies of the book, ***Failed Justice***, please write to the address below:

Please send me _____ copies of your book, Failed Justice. I enclose $15.00 per copy post paid. (If ordering more than 5 copies, please inquire about a discount price.)

Send your order or call: Toll Free: 1-800-528-0371
                                    Fax: 941-643-5243
                                                941-513-9106

Richard Sparkman
Failed Justice
P. O. Box 7128
Naples, FL 34101

Thank you